Powerful Marketing Promos

By

Steven Howard

Powerful Marketing Memos

ISBN: 978-1-943702-02-2 (Print edition)
978-1-943702-03-9 (Kindle edition)

For reprint permission, please contact:
Steven Howard
c/o Caliente Press
1775 E Palm Canyon Drive, Suite 110-198
Palm Springs, CA   92264
U.S.A

Email: steven@howard-marketing.com

Published by:
Caliente Press
1775 E Palm Canyon Drive, Suite 110-198
Palm Springs, CA 92264
U.S.A.

Email: CalientePress@verizon.net

Dedication

This book is dedicated to

Georgette Tan

The best client with whom I have worked.

A client who was truly a partner, in so many ways.

Remarkable projects. Invigorating days. Special memories.

It was always a pleasure working with you.

The following phrases used in this book are trademarked by the author:

If it touches the customer, it's a marketing issue.™

The art of keeping good customers.™

Customer Retention: The Art of Keeping Good Customers™

The Art of Keeping Good Customers.™

Table of Contents

How Customer Values Are Changing

Customer Service

Customer Retention

Corporate Branding

Introduction

Powerful Marketing Memos is a collection of easy-to-read, yet thought-provoking, short essays designed to give corporate leaders, business owners, and entrepreneurs tips on the key marketing topics that will help you grow your businesses, retain customers, and build your corporate brands by:

- Leveraging the organization's most valuable asset — its corporate brand image.

- Creating marketing programs that follow the five Principles of a Customer-Focused Marketing Strategy and incorporate the four cornerstones of Customer Retention.

- Getting the entire organization to concentrate on building, earning, rewarding, and keeping customer loyalty.

These essays are a result of a series of radio presentations I originally created for the program *Positive Business Minutes* in Singapore several years ago. We initially edited and fine-tuned the original 30 broadcasts and added 20 more thoughts and concepts, resulting in one of our early books

Powerful Marketing Minutes: 50 Ways to Develop Market Leadership.

The popularity of these short memos, each with suggest steps for taking action, eventually led to a second book, *MORE Powerful Marketing Minutes: 50 New Ways to Develop Market Leadership.*

As both books are now out of print, and with a new generation of organizational leaders, marketers, business owners, and entrepreneurs struggling with some of the same timeless marketing issues faced by their predecessors, as well as new ones created by the Internet and social media, I felt it was time to bring these memos and thought starters back to life.

Slightly edited, revised, and updated as needed, the 60 *Powerful Marketing Memo* essays in this book discuss a wide range of diverse topics, including corporate branding, customer retention, marketing strategies, customer service, and the changing customer values taking place in today's highly competitive markets.

Each essay is based on my personal philosophy of marketing: ***it it touches the customer, it's a marketing issue.***™ The importance of being customer-focused is reflected in the book's first essay: *A Passion for Customers* and in the later essays on the *Importance of Customer Retention* and *Customer Retention: The Art of Keeping Good Customers.*™

We have purposely kept the writing style lose and friendly, in keeping with the original format in which the concepts were presented on radio. Each essay highlights a specific topic to reflect upon and we encourage the reader to contemplate what changes your organization might require in order to implement the ideas and concepts presented.

Some organizational leaders and business owners will want to use these essays as a personal or senior management daily thought starter, while others will choose to circulate the ideas throughout the organization on a weekly or biweekly basis. Others may prefer to include selected topics on their weekly or monthly management, sales team, or staff meetings.

However you choose to use these essays, we are confident that they will serve you well in creating the kinds of customer-focused, relationship-building marketing activities that are required for success in today's ultra-competitive markets.

Steven Howard

July 2015

A Passion for Customers

Create customer intensity everywhere.

That was the message Lew Platt communicated to his employees when he was CEO at Hewlett-Packard.

And that's the message you should be communicating to your staff, colleagues, and business partners.

Customer intensity should be the core of any customer-focused organization. Personally, I have experienced this only once in my professional working career, when I joined the retail banking division of Citibank in Singapore in 1989. At that time, any meeting at Citibank seemed to have the words *customer* or *customers* as the focal point.

Led by VP and Country Manager David A. Smith at the time, Citibank developed a stellar reputation in Singapore for customer service, innovation, and rapid response to individual customer needs. It was fun and exciting to be both a Citibank employee and a Citibank customer.

Alas, a few years later David moved on to a bigger market and larger challenges, and his replacement had a focus on cost-cutting, operations, and financial management. The topic at meetings turned to numbers, numbers, and more numbers. Changes were made in how customers interacted with the bank and both service and delivery channels became less personalized.

Soon, as both staff and customers started leaving, competitors started to improve their customer focus, and Citibank's leadership position in the Singapore market deteriorated.

Like so many other organizations, Citibank in Singapore in the mid 1990s lost sight of the fact that, as Bradley T. Gale wrote in *Managing Customer Value*, "Companies succeed by providing superior customer value. And value is simply quality, however *the customer* defines it, offered at the right price."

There are three strategies for creating value for customers:

1. Have a true passion for customers.

2. Organize around customers.

3. Cultivate a deep understanding of customers and their *unique* needs, wants, desires, likes and dislikes.

The purpose of business, as the legendary Peter Drucker wrote, is "to create a customer." An updated version would read, "The ultimate role of marketing is to create and keep good customers, to the benefit of customers, the organization, and stakeholders."

Business is not just about sales, contracts, cash flow, internal rates of return, and profitability. Even Henry Ford recognized this when he said, "A business that makes nothing but money is a poor kind of business."

Business leaders need to have the kind of attitude that Louis V. Gerstner had when he was CEO at IBM. When he was first shown an early version of an integrated computer network that became known as the Internet, Gerstner reportedly said, "This is great, this is a new channel for business. How do we make it real for customers? How do we make money on it?"

Note the order of Gerstner's questions. Instinctively he wanted first to know "how to make it real for customers." Then he asked "how do we make money on it?"

This is a CEO exhibiting a true passion for customers by asking how his organization can understand the needs of customers in order to make this new technology real for them. Through his questions, Gerstner was creating customer intensity in his scientists, researchers, and technical staff — not just in his sales, marketing, customer service, and frontline workforce.

Successful companies today are switching from a transaction perspective with their customers to a customer loyalty-building perspective. The way to do this is to earn customer loyalty by understanding true customer needs, committing to quality, delivering upon the promises you make, and by treating customers as people, not as accounts.

In the past, being customer-oriented has meant operating in order to meet the needs of the *typical* customer, or the average customer.

Fewer and fewer businesses today can afford to focus on the average customer. Your future growth, and future profitability, comes from satisfying the needs of your most valuable customers.

To treat your most valuable customers *not as average customers*, but as *your most valued customers*, requires that they be treated as individuals — with individual needs, wants, desires, likes, and dislikes.

This is the true essence behind my concept of *the art of keeping good customers.*™

Key Point: companies succeed by providing superior value, as defined by the customer.

Taking Action: what are you doing _today_ to create customer intensity among your peers, colleagues, and subordinates?

What is the focus of your internal meetings? Numbers or customers? Sales results or customer needs? Statistics or customer inputs? How can you spend more time discussing customers and their needs and less time discussing other matters?

Are you more interested in making money, or making your products and services real for customers? What would it take to have a greater focus on the latter?

How do you reward those in the organization that exhibit high levels of customer intensity? How do you publicize their efforts internally? What can be done to improve these areas and turn your customer-focused folks into internal heroes?

A New Definition of Marketing

It is with shock and horror that I read recently that an Australian Marketing Institute white paper titled *What Value Marketing?* describes "the ultimate role of marketing as delivering increased shareholder value."

When and how did our profession get so far off the mark?

Contrast this with the new definition of marketing from the American Marketing Association, unveiled in the middle of last year:

> *"Marketing is an organizational function and a set of processes for creating, communicating and delivering value to customers and for managing customer relationships in ways that benefit the organization and its stakeholders."*

It's rather sad that even the American Marketing Association (AMA) definition talks about managing customer relationships only in terms of benefits to the organization and its stakeholders. After all, if the customer doesn't benefit from the relationship, I can guarantee you the relationship will not last very long.

Using the new American Marketing Association version as a base, my preferred definition of marketing has become:

> *"The ultimate role of marketing is to create and keep good customers, to the benefit of customers, the organization, and stakeholders."*

As I have written before, business is not just about sales, contracts, cash flow, internal rates of return, and profitability. Even Henry Ford recognized this when he said, "A business that makes nothing but money is a poor kind of business."

Marketing — as an ethos and a philosophy for doing business — is central for the survival and prosperity of any organization. This is why it is far too important to be left to only a handful of marketing specialists.

Marketing must permeate the entire organization and is not something that should be seen as either a "top-down" or a "bottom-up" approach. Rather it must become an approach that infuses and ignites the whole organization.

This inculcation and indoctrination of marketing as a philosophy for doing business, combined with the emphasis on understanding customer needs and creating value for customers, must be led by the top of the organization.

Too many CEOs and other senior executives these days see their primary roles as cutter of costs and manipulators of financial figures. Those duties are best carried out by the Chief Operating Officer. A CEO can better serve his or her customers, employees, communities, shareholders, and board (please note the sequential order of these constituents) by being the guardian of the corporate brand, the motivator of marketing excellence, and the champion of understanding customer needs.

Likewise, marketing also needs to become a central concern of Boards of Directors. Here's what William Parrett, Chief Executive at Deloitte Touche Tohmatsu, wrote in the December 11, 2004 issue of *The Economist*:

> *"A recent survey by Deloitte and the Economist Intelligence Unit found that management and boards of directors focus far too much on financial results that*

represent lagging indicators of past performance. We believe they should pay far more attention to non-financial factors such as customer satisfaction, product and service quality, operational performance, and employee commitment — leading indicators of future performance that firms can use to navigate confidently toward a sustainable future. We also encourage corporate management to communicate with stakeholders about these indicators in quarterly and annual reports."

The winners in this next segment of the economic cycle are not going to be the cost cutters and the retrenchers. The winners are going to be the marketing innovators and the ones who create, protect, and enhance the values customers receive and perceive from transacting business with them and from being associated with them.

It is not only your sales force that must create value for your customers. It is your entire organization. Our personal marketing philosophy is *if it touches the customer, it's a marketing issue.*™

Everything your organization does *touches your customers and your prospects*. Hence, everything you do not only is marketing related, but also impacts the results of your marketing efforts.

In short, everything you do should be done to create value for customers.

This is how you create and keep good customers. Creating and keeping good customers will enable your organization to achieve its bottom-line financial goals, and to increase shareholder value.

But you have to take care of your customers first. As Lee Iacocca, former Chairman and CEO of Chrysler, is quoted as saying "If you take care of your customers, everything else will fall into place."

And that is why my definition of marketing is focused on customers first, the organization second, and shareholders third.

Key Point: the ultimate role of marketing is to create and keep good customers, to the benefit of customers, the organization, and stakeholders.

Taking Action: review your mission statement. Is the emphasis on your customers, the organization, employees, or shareholders? If the answer is anything other than customers, now would be a good time to create a new mission statement.

How involved is your Board in your marketing activities? What steps can be taken to get the Board more interested in marketing and other leading-edge factors such as customer satisfaction, product and service quality, operational performance, and employee commitment?

What role does marketing play in your organization? Is it confined to a solitary functional department? What would it take to create a marketing ethos that permeates throughout your entire organization?

More Thoughts on the Definition of Marketing

In an earlier *Powerful Marketing Memo*, we offered the following as a new definition for marketing:

> *"The ultimate role of marketing is to create and keep good customers, to the benefit of customers, the organization, and stakeholders."*

When I first proposed this new definition of marketing in my *Monday Morning Marketing Memo* newsletter, many readers responded with thought-provoking responses, a few of which I would like to share with you.

Susan Ward from The Chartered Institute of Marketing wrote that "It is my belief that CIM's widely used definition still holds true:

> *"Marketing is the management process responsible for identifying, anticipating and satisfying customer requirements profitably."*

She adds, "Customer relationships will not last long if the company is only in that relationship for its own ends. However, I don't believe that the relationship would last very long if the customer was given exactly what they wanted at any cost to the business. In that situation, it could be said that customers want excellent quality products and service at low prices. Not many companies would stay in business if that was how they operated. The definition given by CIM aims to give a balance between all stakeholders, including customers, recognizing that their requirements are indeed paramount — but crucially, it conveys that the reason a company is in business is to make profits."

While the CIM definition is definitely better than either of the definitions proffered by the American Marketing Association and the Australian Marketing Institute (both cited in the previous memo *A New Definition of Marketing*), the emphasis on profits is a bit bothersome to me. After all, marketing is not something that is limited to just corporations.

This focus on profitability by CIM limits the application of their definition to non-profit organizations, statutory bodies, and government entities, none of which engage the principles and techniques of marketing in order to make profits.

Jacques Chevron, from JRC&A Consulting in Canada wrote, "The head of Caterpillar in France told me many years ago that *'marketing is a state of mind.'* I am still not sure of what he meant exactly but I am increasingly convinced of the statement's wisdom."

I think Jenny Bigio, Managing Director at Write-Angles in Singapore, may understand what the head of Caterpillar meant. She wrote, "It seems that marketing has been hijacked entirely by the left brain — coldly rational, logical, and calculating. Your definition harnesses the right brain's warmth, creativity, sensitivity, intuition. If today's number-crunching managers are living in the past (figures revealing performance) or the future (forecasting), your vision for marketing's role brings balance, so that marketers harness the 'power of now,' being in the present, and totally tuned into their customers and the circumstances in which they operate.

Jenny adds eloquence to my definition, but then again I am probably more "left brained" than her, since she owns and operates a highly successful graphics design and advertising company.

Whether marketing is a state of mind, a deep-seated philosophy, or an ethos for the way one conducts business and interacts with customers is a subject best left for another day.

Successful marketing — and by that I mean highly effective and efficient marketing practices that produce solid, long-term results — is certainly the result of a proper mindset. To me, this proper mindset focuses on customers first, the organization second, and shareholders third.

Many thanks to Susan, Jacques, Jenny, and many others for their inputs. Their thoughts, words, and ideas have given me a reason to pause and reflect on what it is that marketing is all about.

And that's what I hope to accomplish with our readership with each of these *Powerful Marketing Memos* and our associated book *The Best of the Monday Morning Marketing Memo*.

Key Point: the ultimate role of marketing is to create and keep good customers, to the benefit of customers, the organization, and stakeholders.

Taking Action: review your mission statement. Is the emphasis on your customers, the organization, employees, or shareholders? If the answer is anything other than your customers, now would be a good time to create a new mission statement.

How involved is your Board in your marketing activities? What steps can be taken to get the Board more interested in marketing and other leading-edge factors such as customer satisfaction, product and service quality, operational performance, and employee commitment?

What role does marketing play in your organization? Is it confined to a solitary functional department? What would it take to create a marketing ethos that permeates throughout your entire organization?

12 Marketing Philosophies

I thought I would share with you 12 of my personal marketing philosophies that will enable each *Powerful Marketing Memo* reader to develop his or her own beliefs on the fundamentals of marketing.

In no particular order of importance, these 12 marketing philosophies are:

1. Segment customers based on customer needs, not the needs of your organization and not based around the structures of your existing organizational chart.

2. In order for customers to see you as a unique brand or service provider, you need to treat them as unique individuals — with individually unique needs, wants, desires, likes, and dislikes.

3. Remember that when dealing with customers (even in the B2B world) you are dealing with fellow human beings, not revenue streams. Thus, every customer matters and every customer interaction matters (especially to the customer).

4. The era of mass production required mass communications. Today's era of *individual* customers and smaller customer segments requires a more individualized approach to marketing communications.

5. Your fellow employees communicate your brand's true value to customers. Every employee interaction with a customer or prospect, therefore, either enhances or denigrates your brand reputation and the customer's brand experience.

6. With the increased importance to customers of Corporate Social Responsibility, your corporate image is more important than ever. How your corporate image is managed is critical. After all, competitors can replicate your products and services, beat you up on price, outspend you in promotions, and outperform you in distribution. However, the one thing competitors cannot copy or duplicate is a well-defined, well-managed corporate image.

7. The Four Ps of Customer Retention (People, Policies, Processes and Procedures, and Prevention) are more relevant for retaining customers captured through the time honored marketing mix than the original Four Ps of marketing created 40 years ago by Professor Kotler. (See chapters 41 and 42 of my book *The Best of the Monday Morning Marketing Memo* for details on the 4 Ps of Customer Retention.)

8. It is not what you communicate, it is what your customers hear that is most important. Customers have learned how to filter out traditional marketing messages and have the tools to do so. Getting customers to *hear* your marketing messages requires greater creativity, increased innovation, more relevance, and heightened integration.

9. Profitability is not very useful or informative for understanding customer needs.

10. Focus on your customers and their needs, wants, desires, likes, and dislikes. Remember, if you don't take care of your customers, someone else will.

11. CRM works better when it means Customer Retention Marketing. Customer Retention is *the art of keeping good customers*™ and should be the cornerstone foundation for all long-term marketing strategies.

12. *If it touches the customer, it's a marketing issue.*™ Marketing is *the* critical integrator across all business lines and all internal departments.

I hope you are able to put some, if not all, of the above marketing philosophies into practice.

Key Point: *if it touches the customer, it's a marketing issue.*™

Taking Action: what are your own personal marketing philosophies? How do these impact the short-term and long-term decisions you make?

Circulate the above list to your staff or fellow colleagues. Discuss which ones instinctively feel right for your organization. Why? How could these be disseminated widely throughout your department, business unit, or entire organization?

No Such Thing as a Commodity Product

Product differentiation is a marketing technique that can be applied to any product or service offer.

It is my deep-seated belief that *there is no such thing as a commodity product....there are only products that are marketed like commodities.*

Remember the second customer-focused marketing principle? *Customers do not buy products — they buy solutions.* One way to differentiate your product is through the way it provides solutions. Another is through the "total customer experience" that it provides.

One of the best marketing articles I ever read came from the global consultants Booz Allen & Hamilton, and was titled *How to Brand Sand.* It gave a case example of a company that turned sand into silicon, gave it a brand name, and captured a huge portion of its market by becoming the industry standard....even though the characteristics and technical specifications of the product were no different than the other silicon products offered by competitors.

One of my favorite marketing stories is about a sales person at Ciba Specialty Chemicals who was selling pigment to a paint manufacturer in Taiwan.

Now the pigments that go into paint are about as close to a commodity product as one will find.

These pigments are sold within the industry in 30 kilo bags and shipped in large palletized lots. The salesman found out that his customer was using 75 kilos of this particular pigment in every batch run. Thus, the customer was using 2½ bags of the pigment, which meant that half a bag needed to be stored somewhere until the next batch run.

The salesman worked with Ciba's bag manufacturer, and his own internal manufacturing and shipping people, and learned that it was possible to have 25 kilo bags made and palletized.

Now, for this particular customer, Ciba ships this pigment in 25 kilo bags and the customer no longer has to measure out half bag allotments nor store half bags of pigment.

The result: Ciba Specialty Chemicals now has almost 100% customer share with this particular customer because they found a way to meet the individual and specific needs of their customer with a unique solution.

Through an innovative packaging technique, Ciba found a way to differentiate paint pigment.

Surely you can find a way to differentiate your own products and services.

Key Point: there is no such thing as a commodity product — there are only products that are marketed like commodities.

Taking Action: describe the "total customer experience" for your products. How does this differ from that of your competitors?

Where are the opportunities to differentiate your product *in a way that such differentiation is meaningful to your customers*? Can this differentiation be made in packaging? Product enhancements? Facets of delivery? Your sales terms and conditions?

Does your staff believe you are selling a commodity or that you're in a commodity industry?

Brands and Customers are Hidden Assets

A goal of every organization is to increase its assets over time. These assets are typically defined in terms of revenue, customer accounts, properties, human resources, and capital.

But there are two hidden assets that every organization can develop and that are critical for marketing success. These often overlooked and under-valued assets are the brands and customers.

Your brands, particularly your corporate brand, can be highly valuable assets....for these serve as trust marks between you and your customers. Why is a brand an asset? Quite simply because the central essence of a brand is a promise....a promise of consistency, reliability, and satisfaction.

A brand is more than just a trademark, or the name on your building. A brand, especially your corporate brand, is an asset that has meaning and enormous financial value. Years ago RJR Nabisco was purchased for almost twice its book value. The difference between its book value and the price paid was the buyer's understanding of the value of the RJR Nabisco brands like Oreo cookies, Camel cigarettes, and Ritz crackers.

More recently, Ford paid seven times sales to purchase Jaguar. It certainly wasn't for the Jaguar factory. It was because Ford wanted a premium brand, a premium brand with value, in its portfolio.

If you treat your brand like an asset, and develop it over time, your payoff will come today in terms of higher repeat sales and more loyal customers, and in the long term from a higher valuation of your company over book value.

The other under-valued asset in your portfolio is your customer base.

Successful companies today are switching from a transaction perspective with their customers to a customer loyalty-building perspective. The way to do this is to earn customer loyalty, by understanding true customer needs, committing to quality, delivering upon the promises you make, and by treating customers as people, not as accounts.

Three key areas you should be questioning your organization include:

- Does our organization *respect* our customers and prospects....or do we see them in terms of the transactions they make with us?

- Do we *appreciate* that our customers seek convenience and do we have the processes in place that enhance convenience to our customers?

- Are we in the business of solving problems for our customers, or merely in the business of making products and hoping that someone purchases these?

Your corporate brand and your customers are two of the most important assets you have. What are you doing today to enhance the value of these two assets? That's a question worth considering each and every day.

Key Point: your corporate brand and your customers are two of the most important assets you have.

Taking Action: how does your organization show its respect for customers? Are these efforts recognized and appreciated by your customers?

What can you do to make the buying process more convenient for customers?

What can you do to make your service delivery more convenient for customers?

Is "convenience delivery" an opportunity for differentiation in your industry?

What are you doing to increase the value of your brand and customer assets?

Marketing Excellence

Through the years, the marketing process has evolved from one art form to another.

As more and more companies are now competing on a global basis, and as customers around the globe become more knowledgeable and have more options to choose from, organizations need to raise their marketing prowess and speed up their progression along this marketing excellence road path if they are to win future marketing battles.

Recent trends in marketing can be broadly classified as:

Product Excellence

Product Positioning and Branding Excellence

Service Excellence

Distribution Excellence

Dialogue Excellence

My projection is that the next level of marketing excellence will be seen in the field of Relationship Excellence.

This is an admitted over-simplification of the evolution of marketing excellence because some companies, and even some countries, have either been ahead or behind these trends.

Also, this evolution does not always occur in a linear fashion.

For instance, Singapore Airlines began the rise of service excellence within the airline industry in the 1970s, well ahead of its competitors. On the other hand, Qantas Airways redefined product excellence in the airline industry in the 1980s when it became the first to offer a Business Class section.

However, after the proliferation of Business Class cabins across every major international airline by the end of the 1980s, SIA took the marketing process a step further by branding its Business Class service as Raffles Class.

In general though, all industries and markets go through this evolutionary progression from product excellence to branding and distribution excellence, and onto dialogue excellence.

For instance, in every industry there is a time when high levels of commercial success are practically guaranteed simply by manufacturing and distributing an innovative or very good product.

However, once a plethora of competitors has entered a field or product category, product excellence alone is no longer sufficient to ensure marketing success. Thus comes the need to develop brand names and personalities in order to differentiate one product from another.

Then, the marketing environment progresses to a stage where product excellence and distinct brand personalities are no longer the key, or sole, factors in the purchase decision-making process. At this stage, customers begin to demand excellent service in addition to high quality product features and associated personalities.

One critical aspect of service excellence is customer convenience. Winning the marketing battle by providing the highest levels of convenience to customers is a critical determining factor in the stage of distribution excellence.

Once high levels of service and distribution excellence are reached within an industry, such as the hotel industry in Asia, the market share leader will be the organization that develops the highest level of dialogue excellence with its customer base.

Now I would agree with the many consumers who find a lack of dialogue excellence in today's markets, but at least a start has been made by some service providers. Many organizations have begun to develop two-way communications processes with key customers in order to continuously monitor customer needs and to customize product and service offers.

Unfortunately, many of these initiatives have been bastardized by organizations more interested in simply tracking customer purchasing behaviors and by inept attempts to develop so-called "loyalty marketing" programs. The latter are often poorly disguised attempts to buy loyalty through reward schemes and bonus point systems that have as much to do with loyalty building as coupons and discount cards.

Dialogue excellence is merely the first stage on the path to relationship excellence. Unfortunately, many organizations get stuck at this point and fail to progress (partly because of a belief that customer relationships can be *managed*.)

However, for those companies who have understood how to make it easy for customers to communicate *with* them, the world is literally beating a path to their stores and other buying channels. And, as long as the other elements of marketing excellence are maintained and faultlessly delivered, the opportunity for bi-mutual, solid *relationship excellence* with customers becomes available.

Key Point: marketing excellence is an art that evolves through several stages from product excellence to relationship excellence.

Taking Action: in which stage of marketing excellence are you competing today? How can you move up to the next level?

What resources would be required to add superior service to a strategy that is grounded in product positioning or branding excellence? What would be needed to evolve from service excellence to dialogue excellence?

Convenience is a key concern for customers today. How can your distribution strategy incorporate added convenience for customers?

Dialogue Excellence Leads to Relationship Excellence

As organizations move from dealing with people in general to dealing with individuals as unique customers, the role of communications becomes ever more important.

We have reached an era where dialogue excellence is not only feasible, but it is becoming mandatory for our relationship-building efforts with customers and all other key organizational constituents: employees, shareholders, the financial community, the media, local community groups, customers, prospects, and partners.

Dialogue excellence links the product, marketing, and service excellence stages with the relationship marketing stage. A successful relationship, for both organizations and individuals, can only be formed through excellent dialogue skills. If you cannot communicate clearly, openly, and honestly with one another, there is no chance for the development of a meaningful relationship.

We understand this instinctively when it comes to forming and maintaining interpersonal relationships.

The same holds true for relationships between organizations, and between organizations and people.

Hence, not many organizations are fully ready for relationship excellence, as they have yet to fulfill the requirements of dialogue excellence.

I stated earlier my belief that the next stage of marketing excellence, the stage that follows distribution excellence and dialogue excellence, will be in the field of relationship excellence.

I truly feel that relationship marketing will be one of the key success factors in the next couple of decades. We have already begun to move from mass marketing to mass customization (e.g. customized jeans from Levi Strauss) in many sectors and industries. This individualized marketing is one of the unique aspects of relationship marketing.

The credit card industry is one that readily moved from dialogue excellence to relationship excellence. Let's look at how this industry has evolved through the various stages of marketing excellence.

The Gold MasterCard, created by MasterCard International in 1981, was the first bank credit card created especially for a higher income market segment. The product allowed customers to tell their banks that they desired a credit card with a higher credit line or one with enhanced services over the bank's standard level card. Hence, product positioning excellence was combined with service excellence.

This product segmentation approach was taken a step further with the introduction of co-branded and affinity card programs, such as the General Motors MasterCard, the American Airlines AAdvantage MasterCard, and the HongkongBank Care for Nature MasterCard programs. By choosing affinity or co-branded credit card programs, consumers identify and align themselves with programs and organizations they desire to support. These programs are conceived and created through dialogue excellence skills that helped to identify and quantify the types of co-branded and affinity relationships that would be most meaningful to cardholders (and thus would result in the highest number of credit cards issued).

Freedom of choice is becoming the way of the world as customers find opportunities to buy products and services from beyond their normal geographic or product scopes. These decisions are going to be based as much on the perceived relationships the customers have with the supplying organizations as on product characteristics, brand personalities, price, and delivery convenience.

Think about it — if we are entering a world of parity products, parity branding, parity pricing, and parity distribution, what factors are left for customers to use in deciding which products and services to purchase? The answer comes down to two highly interlinked factors: the relationship between the customer and the providing organization, and the perceived corporate image of the organization.

Key Point #1: dialogue excellence is a prerequisite for relationship excellence.

Key Point #2: moving from mass marketing to mass customization is one way of moving to relationship marketing excellence.

Taking Action: review your communications activities with key constituents. Are these one-way messages aimed at passive consumers or the "mass market"? How can your messages be more tailored so that you are communicating with individuals as unique customers?

When was the last time you audited the communications activities of your competitors? Have they moved past you into the stage of dialogue excellence? If not, how can you get there first?

Is your Internet strategy nothing more than an electronic form of one-way communications? How can your website encourage greater dialogue with its visitors?

What are the opportunities for providing mass customization of your product offer? What options, choices, and flexibility can be built into your products?

How can your customers be enlisted to create their own customized versions of your products?

If your industry is currently competing on service excellence, how can you get to dialogue excellence first? If you are in the early stages of competing on dialogue excellence, what will it take for you to reach relationship excellence first?

The Customer Is King

We live in a world of change. As a matter of fact, the rate of change today is faster, and affects a larger portion of the earth's population, than at any other time in history. And, as some pundits like to repeat, "The only thing constant in our lives is change."

One constant, however, remains: for all organizations, big or small, start-ups or fast growing, profit or non-profit, marketing-driven and customer-centric approaches are required to generate any level of sustainable success.

My personal market-driven philosophy is *if it touches the customer, it's a marketing issue.*™

Anything that touches your customers....that impacts your customers or your prospects....should be considered a marketing issue for your entire organization.

This marketing philosophy has led me to develop five customer-driven marketing strategies. Let me share the first one with you.

I call it the **golden rule of marketing**: **the customer is king**.

No, the customer is *not* always right. But the customer is still the customer, at all times. And as marketers and business leaders, it is imperative that we fully understand and appreciate the needs of each and every one of our customers.

Thus, it is mandatory that everyone in the organization who has contact with customers and prospects be taught how to investigate customer wants and needs. And, they need to be able to *fully understand and appreciate* these needs.

Then, your company needs to determine how it can best serve the needs of these customers....profitably, efficiently, and consistently.

Bear in mind, of course, that it will be your customers who are the judges of how well your organizations satisfy their requirements. Your internal measures don't really matter, unless you are using the same measurement yardsticks as your customers.

I recall when I first joined a major international retail bank. On the first week on the job I was invited to a party, in celebration of the fact that the bank had just exceeded its own goals on the issuance of ATM cards to new account holders. The bank had achieved a 94%

level of issuing these cards within seven days of new account openings for the previous month. It was the first time the team had surpassed the goal of 92%.

"Wonderful," I thought. "We are willing to set a goal that leaves 8% of our customers less than satisfied." However, not wanting to damper the spirits of the team, I kept my initial thoughts to myself.

Later I enquired whether we had ever asked customers if seven days was satisfactory in their minds. Unfortunately, the reply I got was "no." Hence, I made sure that in our next regular customer satisfaction survey we included a question on "how many days should it take for you to receive your ATM card after you open up a new account with us?"

As I recall, something like 85% of the respondents selected either three days or four days in response to this question. Hence, not only were we will to live with a statistical service measurement that said it was okay to not satisfy 8% of our new customers.....we didn't have a clue (until the research findings) that in fact we were actually disappointing the large majority of customers by using a measurement criteria that was not in tune with their own thinking.

Please remember, while the customer may not always be right, he or she is still the customer.

And in their hands lie the future fate of your businesses.

Key Point: your customers are the judges of how well your organizations satisfy their requirements. Internal measures don't really matter, unless you are using the same measurement yardsticks as your customers and have a full understanding of customer expectations on service delivery.

Taking Action: ask your senior managers to brainstorm and develop a list of the things your organization tracks in relationship to customer satisfaction.

When was the last time you checked these measurement yardsticks against the requirements of your customers? If it's been awhile, you should make it a high priority to conduct a Customer Satisfaction Survey with your existing clients and ask them how you are doing in fully meeting their needs.

Customers Do Not Buy Products

There are five key customer-driven marketing principles that I consider critical to marketing success today.

The first is that the customer is king. The second is: *customers do not buy products....they buy solutions.*

Hence, it is important that you and your entire organization think of your products and services in terms of the solutions they provide to your customers.

For example, a person doesn't need a quarter-inch drill. That person *needs* a quarter-inch hole made. This hole can be made several different ways, only one of which is using a drill.

By thinking of your products as solutions, you won't get surprised by unexpected competition that emerges from outside your industry.

For instance, there used to be a company that made the best slide rules in the world. That company is out of business today....not beaten by the likes of another slide rule company....but totally defeated by Hewlett-Packard and Texas Instruments as these technology giants developed electronic calculators that performed scientific equations faster and more reliably than slide rules.

Likewise, if you were a manufacturer of lawn mowers, you would have to be concerned by the life sciences company Monsanto, which has developed a grass seed that grows grass exactly one inch high. If a customer, such as a golf course or a public park, wants one-inch high grass, the *solution* they may decide upon could just as easily be the purchase and use of this innovative grass seed from Monsanto, rather than the purchase of lawn mowers and the hiring of crews to cut the grass every month or every fortnight.

When you think of your own products and services as solutions, you'll be in a better strategic position to remember that your customers are looking for the benefits they get in purchasing, using, or consuming your products or services.

Customers buy solutions....not products.

Key Point: customers look at your products and services as potential solutions to their problems or opportunities. So should you.

Taking Action: go through your key products and services. What solutions are these providing to your customers? What customer problems are they NOT solving?

Could you possibly extend your product or service offer to solve these other customer problems, thereby creating additional value-added components to your current products or services?

Marketing is Critical to Survival

We have previously discussed the first two of the five customer-driven marketing strategies.

Let us focus on the third one now. The third customer-focused marketing strategy is that: *marketing is too important to be left only to the marketing department.*

Marketing — as an ethos and a philosophy for doing business — is central to the survival and prosperity of your organization. This is why it is far too important to be left to only a handful of marketing specialists.

Everyone in your organization should be taught my simple marketing philosophy — *if it touches the customer, it's a marketing issue.*™

Anything and everything that touches your customers is a marketing issue because these issues are what the customer will use in deciding whether to do business with you, or whether to continue doing business with you.

Remember, the customer is the *raison d'être* for your business.

Frontline customer service is important, but so is your back-room processing performance, statements and invoicing, policies, delivery schedules, and everything else that has a direct impact on customers.

It will do your organization little good to have smiling, helpful, and efficient frontline service people, if the attitude within the rest of the organization is that customers are a pain and are too demanding in their requests.

Also, marketing departments often worry too much about data collection, market share, and other items that have very little impact on your customers or on your products and services.

I encourage you to make market share a secondary concern. The important criterion to focus on is customer share (particularly for the higher profit segment of your customer base).

And the best way to ensure that you are getting as much customer share as possible is to ensure that your entire organization has a customer-focused, marketing-led culture that understands the real reason you are in business today is to create and keep customers.

Key Point: the reason you are in business today is to create and keep customers.

Taking Action: who is responsible for marketing in your organization? If the answer is not "everybody," then you do not have a marketing-driven ethos.

What are your customer "touch points?" Are these touch points customer-focused or process driven?

What level of customer share are you capturing from your top customers? How could this be improved?

What would happen to your business if 10% of your top customers left? What might cause them to leave?

Remembering that an ounce of prevention is worth a pound of cure, what can you put into place now to prevent those top customers from departing?

Markets Are Heterogeneous

Of the five customer-driven marketing strategies that I recommend to you, the fourth principle is the one that today's leading marketing organizations have taken to heart most deeply.

This fourth principle is: *markets are heterogeneous. They are not homogeneous.*

Customers are all different individuals....with different needs, wants, desires, likes, and dislikes. We can no longer make the mistake of treating all customers as if they are the same.

Sure, it is still important to classify customers according to subgroups and segments. But that is mostly for communications purposes so that your limited advertising, promotions, and marketing budgets can be stretched to their fullest.

But when it comes to dealing with customers at each point of interaction....it is important to deal with them as individuals....not as account numbers....and certainly not as unknown entities whose requests we want to process just as fast as possible so that we can go on to the next unknown entity.

Customers today want, they demand actually, flexibility and customization from their service and product providers. The more flexibility and customization you can build into your product and service offers, the brighter your future will be.

The Internet is changing the way people think and the way they experience other products and services. You should not be surprised when your customers bring this thinking....and a new set of expectations based on their experiences elsewhere....with them when they deal with you and your organization.

The Internet is enabling smart marketers, like Amazon, United Airlines, Avis, and Charles Schwab, to personalize and customize the buying experience for their customers.

The more you can interact with your customers on a one-to-one basis, the greater are the chances that you will be able to completely satisfy the needs of these customers.

Success is a simple equation: customer satisfaction results in repeat purchases....and repeat purchases result in customer loyalty.

Building your business on creating customer loyalty is one of the best business models you can use.

Key Point: customers today want, and demand, customization and flexibility from their product and service providers.

Taking Action: do your customers see your product and service offers as having built-in customization options and flexibility?

How about your policies? Are they rigid and rigorous or do your employees have the power to modify these to meet specific and particular customer needs?

At each point of interaction, are your customers recognized and treated as individuals? Would I be recognized as a repeat visitor to your website, or treated just like any other person? (For a good example of how this can be done, transact at Amazon.)

What do your competitors do in terms of being flexible?

How can you make each point of interaction more personable and rewarding for your customers?

How can you enhance customer loyalty and use this as the cornerstone of your business model?

Markets and Customers are Constantly Changing

In previous essays I have given you the first four customer-driven marketing strategies.

Let's look at the fifth, and final, customer-driven marketing principle, which is: *markets and customers are constantly changing.*

This should come as a surprise to no one. We are living in a world where product obsolescence occurs quicker than ever before. In a world where new technologies and new products are becoming an almost daily occurrence. In a world where the commercialization of new technologies and new products is happening faster than before. And in a world where people are adapting to new technology and new product features quicker than ever.

It is important for all of us to remember that markets are dynamic....and that products today often have a shorter shelf life than before.

Do you remember the electronic typewriter of the mid 1980s? Portable....or perhaps I should say luggable....typewriters that used thermal paper. A great concept in their time, but completely replaced today by the notebook computers and tablets.

And who's to say that the notebook computer will last forever? I see many people now using their tablets and iPads to perform many of the functions I use my own notebook computer for.

How will this accelerated rate of change affect your business?

That's a question you and your senior executives should probably be asking yourself every day.

Key Point: the rate of change and of consumer adoption of new technology is increasingly faster.

Taking Action: how will this accelerated rate of change affect your business?

What can you do to keep your employees aware of changes in the market place? How well do you adapt new technologies?

What new product or service could be a threat to your business? How could you implement a new technology to create a competitive edge for your business?

Loyalty Building

An interesting phenomena that we see in the world of marketing today is that companies are switching from a transaction perspective to a loyalty-building perspective....at least when it comes to their best (and most profitable) customers.

There are only three ways to grow your business....and it doesn't matter what business you are in. You can either:

1. Increase the number of your customers.

2. Persuade your current customers to buy in larger volumes.

3. Encourage your current customers to buy more often from you.

So, as you can see....two of the three ways to grow your business....any business....is to concentrate on your current customer base. And, for many businesses, increasing the number of customers also requires a focus on the current customer base as a large percentage of new customers is often generated through referrals made by your current customers.

This means making a dedicated effort to focus on your current customers — and to develop relationship marketing programs, particularly with your key customers — is more important than ever.

By relationship marketing, I don't mean the tactical "loyalty points" programs we see so often in today's markets. While these are very good tactical campaigns, the various bonus points schemes that banks and others use for their loyalty building programs are often no more successful in building long-term customer loyalty than lucky draw promotions.

I remember when a bank in Singapore conducted a Lucky Draw competition for deposit customers with the grand prize being a beautiful new Jaguar automobile. The winner, when asked by a local newspaper if winning this luxury car would make him loyal to the bank providing the prize, replied "No, there's a new promotion at this other bank, so I'm going to try my luck over there now."

It's pretty obvious to me that if you cannot buy customer loyalty by giving away a Jaguar car, then you simply cannot *buy* loyalty.

If you want *true* customer loyalty you have to build it, earn it, and reward it before you can keep customers truly loyal.

Elsewhere in *Powerful Marketing Memos* we give you tips on how to build customer loyalty....how to earn customer loyalty....how to reward customer loyalty....and how to keep customers loyal.

Key Point: true customer loyalty has to be built, earned, and rewarded before customers become truly loyal.

Taking Action: are you and your competitors locked into a series of "promotional wars" with competition down to the best loyalty points scheme?

Are your efforts at loyalty building based on the benefits of your products and services, or based on what types of rewards and freebies you give away?

How easy would it be for a competitor to better your rewards program?

What can your organization do to build and earn customer loyalty? How can your relationship marketing programs be designed around customer needs, especially recurring needs?

Treating Customers Differently

In this series of *Powerful Marketing Memos*, I have written often about the growing need to treat customers as individuals — with individual needs, wants, desires, likes, and dislikes.

There are four steps to go about this, and are detailed in the book *The One to One Fieldbook* by Don Peppers, Martha Rogers, and Bob Dorf.

They identify four key implementation tasks that can be used as a guide for initiating individual relationship marketing programs, or what they call 1:1 marketing. These four steps are:

> **Identify** — identify your customers in as much detail as possible. You need to know more than demographic data like age, address, income. You also need to know their habits, preferences, and reasons for transacting with you. This information needs to be linked across your entire operations.

> **Differentiate your customers** — customers are different in two critical ways:

they each represent a different level of value to the organization and they each have different needs from you. The more you can differentiate your customer base, the better you can prioritize your efforts so that you gain the most advantage with your most valuable customers. Additionally, such differentiation allows you to tailor the organization's behavior to each customer based on that customer's individual needs.

Interact *with* your customers — every interaction with a customer should take place in the context of all previous interactions with that customer. One goal of every interaction with a customer should be to acquire additional information about that customer that can help you make decisions or implement new strategies.

Customize — customize some aspect, or many aspects, of how your organization interacts with and behaves toward each individual customer. In order to practice true 1:1 marketing, the production or service-delivery aspect of your business has to be able to treat a particular customer differently based on what *that customer* said during an interaction with you.

In the past, being customer-oriented has meant operating in order to meet the needs of the *typical* customer, or the average customer.

Fewer and fewer businesses today can afford to focus on the average customer. Your future growth, and future profitability, comes from satisfying the needs of your most valuable customers.

To treat your most valuable customers *not as average customers*, but as your most valued customers, requires that they be treated as individuals — with individual needs, wants, and desires.

This is the true essence of what is often called 1:1 marketing.

Key Point: it is important to treat your customers, particularly your most valuable customers, as individuals with individual wants, needs, and desires.

Taking Action: what are you doing in terms of identifying and tracking your most valuable customers? Do you really know their preferences, likes, and dislikes?

How can you do a better job of differentiating the organization's behavior based on individual needs?

How can you do a better job of disseminating customer-specific information throughout the entire organization so that each customer receives a seamless experience that caters to his or her needs?

What can you do to differentiate and customize your service delivery, especially for your most valuable customers?

Using Technology to Drive Your Business and Build Customer Relationships

From the many journals and articles which this author reads, it appears that the world's senior managers have started to recover from the temporary amnesia caused by their collective flirtations with re-engineering and other "slice the fat" processes, and that a renewed focus on growing their respective businesses has replaced the previous emphasis on cutting costs.

In addition to thinking how to use information technology to roadmap marketing improvements in product differentiation, customer satisfaction, faster and more reliable distribution channels, speedier time-to-market, and/or low-cost production strategies, today's senior managers and business owners also need to contemplate how to migrate to the kinds of relationship excellence strategies that will supersede product excellence and service excellence delivery.

What should senior management be demanding of information technology? The easiest answer is to simply reply: to support the business. The harder task is to figure out what forms this support should take. Even harder still is to know when new and developing technology should be used to *drive the business*, not merely lend support to other business drivers.

Through the years, information technology advances and techniques have been used for transaction processing, data capture, data analysis, and for executive information and executive decision support systems. Since the early part of the 1990s, information technology has also been widely used in the efforts to cut costs, reduce corporate payrolls, and to increase the productivity of the remaining work force.

Today, senior management is beginning to realize that their true job descriptions call for the *growing of businesses* and that for many organizations future profits are only going to come from the implementation of growth strategies. As such, senior managers must re-evaluate what they demand of their information technology investments, particularly in those organizations which are segueing from a cost-restructuring mindset to a corporate culture which emphasizes growth and the capturing of market opportunities.

Getting in front of the technology curve is a worry for most senior management. As Charles V. Callahan and Joseph Nemec Jr. point out in their article *The CEO's Information Technology Agenda,* many CEOs and other senior managers view the world of information technology with "varying degrees of skepticism" — many having been badly burnt by previous big-ticket information technology investments "whose promise has far outweighed the end results."

However, we are constantly seeing global markets and industries transformed rapidly by companies and organizations which have the foresight, courage, and wisdom to drive business growth strategies, and even to create entire new business categories, through the use of information technology.

Examples include First Direct in the United Kingdom, the first bank created without branches (all transactions are conducted by telephone, computer access, ATMs or mail) and the development of Maestro,™ a global on-line point-of-sale debit card program by MasterCard which extended the concept of national EFTPOS networks across borders into the global arena.

It may seem strange to have a marketing person like myself expounding on the glories of investing in information technology. However, I am a big, big believer in using information technology as a key driver of business success and market leadership.

In addition to using information technology to drive business development, as outlined in the previous marketing memo, organizations also need to begin thinking and understanding how to use IT to *drive customer relationships*.

Probably more than any other IT application, this is the one key criterion which senior management must factor into their assessments of their future information technology requirements — the development, maintenance, and retention of customer relationships.

Sir Peter Bonfield, chief executive of British Telecommunications PLC, wrote:

> *"the winners in the information age are going to be those organizations that deploy the new technologies to make themselves*

more efficient and faster than their competitors, that are better at understanding and meeting the needs of their customers, and that constantly look to the future to develop and enrich the ways in which they interact with their customers, partners, suppliers, and employees."

Future marketing success will come to those who understand how to use technology to meet *tomorrow's* customer needs, not to those who spend massive amounts of dollars supporting only today's business requirements.

As written in earlier essays, customers place high value on customization and choices. One route to increasing customization satisfaction will be by providing increased options and choices for customers, without making such choices overly confusing or too difficult to comprehend.

One of the top needs of customers is to have their relationship requirements satisfied. I can think of no better concept or goal for business owners, CEOs and other senior managers to focus on when asking themselves the question, "What should we be demanding of our investments in information technology?"

Strategic investments in technology that will drive your future business growth, rather than just support your existing business, is certainly a bona fide way to develop market leadership.

Key Point: future marketing success will come to those who understand how to use technology to meet *tomorrow's* customer needs, not to those who spend massive amounts of dollars supporting only today's business requirements.

Taking Action: what do you demand as a return for your technology investments? Are these investments focused on driving your future business, developing relationships, or in supporting your current business?

How can your organization do a better job of using technology to better understand and meet the needs of your customers?

How can your organization use technology to develop and enrich the ways in which your staff interact with your customers, partners, suppliers, and employees?

Using Technology to Drive Relationships

The implications of the importance of relationship marketing in the near future for information technology systems and IT managers are enormous.

The two keys related to information technology which will drive relationship excellence in the coming years are:

1) the ability to customize product and service offerings which meet the needs of individuals, and

2) the ability to create higher levels of customer service delivery *by getting customers to perform self-service functions.*

Inherent in the ability to customize product and service offers is the notion that access to information and self-selected ordering systems must be defined from the customer's perspective, which more often these days means convenient access when, where, and how the "I the 24x7 Customer" wants.

Individuals will form relationships with organizations which meet their individual needs, and which have image associations with which the individual wishes to identify with. The latter is a marketing issue subject of discussion elsewhere in *Powerful Marketing Memos*.

Meeting individual needs, particularly the need for customization of the product or service offer, will require heavy use of information technology by organizations to understand, track, and deliver upon each unique customer requirement. The organizations that build their information technology systems around this process are the ones who will undoubtedly win the future battles for customer relationships and customer loyalty.

Levi Strauss is a good example of a company that first used technology to march down the path of mass customization. It was the first retailer that enabled customers to go into a store, get measured for a pair of tailored jeans, and have those jeans delivered within a matter of days.

Levi's uses information technology to send the individual store orders directly to the manufacturing plant, where the measurements are transferred into the machines cutting and sewing the jeans. The information technology system then tracks the shipment of the customized jeans to the store that took the customer's order. Alternatively, the jeans (called Personal Pair) can be shipped via UPS directly to the customer's residence or office. Once the measurements are entered into the Levi's customer database, future orders can be made through the telephone or via the Internet.

Not only does Levi's satisfy the customization needs of its customers, but this process for the Personal Pair products also results in much higher repeat business for Levi's. According to a senior vice president at Levi's, approximately 37% of Personal Pair customers repeat purchases from Levi's, which is over triple the norm.

Unfortunately, the use of technology to drive customer relationships is far from the norm. For the most part, market-driven organizations generally see information technology as a support function, with its main purposes usually being to create:

1) Ease of access to customers.

2) Ease of access for customers (i.e. enhanced distribution methodologies).

3) Greater accuracy and speed at the point of purchase transaction.

4) Faster supply chain management in order to ensure that the distribution pipeline remains optimally stocked at the highest levels of efficiency and the lowest costs possible.

While these are all worthy and worthwhile practices, they are far from the ultimate use of information technology in meeting the needs and the high value criteria of today's demanding and high-expectation customers.

Relationship excellence is projected to be *the* marketing stratagem of the future for many industries, companies, and organizations. As such, these organizations, and many others, will need to demand that their technology information systems have the capability to *drive relationship excellence.*

Key Point: information technology can be used as a strategic tool in developing strong customer relationship programs.

Taking Action: how can information technology be used by your organization to create customized product or service offers?

How can information technology be used by your organization to drive self-service choices and options for your customers?

Is your information technology being used to support today's market-driven culture or tomorrow's customer-centric requirements?

Communications Trend #1

Let us explore some of the significant trends impacting the ability of organizations to communicate to their key audiences effectively and efficiently today.

First, the most important trend is that the entire developed world, and a great part of the developing world, is rapidly moving from a need for content to a desire for context.

While futurologists continue to write about the coming information age, I suggest that much of the world has already entered this era. Today's problem is that there is simply too much raw information and data available. The problem will get worst with the continued proliferation of the Internet and the wide availability of information and the ease of information sharing.

As a result, the need (and challenge) for the immediate future for marketers is to package and deliver *relevant* content in a meaningful and timely manner to both customers and prospects.

In business, we have already seen the types of information systems go from transaction processing systems to knowledge work systems (including computer-aided design). In other words, technology was used first for operational activities and then for knowledge and information gathering.

Today, management information systems support, and sometimes lead, decision making while providing executive information systems that put the core data into an understandable context.

But I am not just talking about the need for "knowledge workers" in tomorrow's growth industries either. Customers are going through the same information transition. Very few organizations deal with uniformed customers these days (though your frontline and customer service staff may not always agree with that statement).

The market today comprises intelligent, demanding customers who have the mobility and the freedom of movement to go elsewhere if their rational and emotional needs are not met. At the same time, all of us are bombarded with thousands of marketing messages **every day**. These messages are contributing to a feeling of information overload, resulting in many marketing communications messages going undigested or barely noticed.

What does this mean to you as an organization trying to get your message across to your intended audiences?

It means that you are going to have to do a much better job of communicating to your target audiences *the context* of your message and *why your messages are relevant and important to the recipient.*

Those who do not will find their customer bases dwindling and their efforts at relationship development fraught with disappointments.

Informed customers no longer need more information and raw data, they need information put into a tangible, pertinent, and usable format.

A second important trend impacting the communications process is that a huge disintegration gap is developing between the marketing communications messages being sent by organizations and the comprehension of these messages by customers. That will be the topic of our next essay in *Powerful Marketing Memos* on the following pages.

In the meantime, please remember to start tailoring your marketing communications into context that can be more readily understood and appreciated by your audiences.

Key Point: your audiences need you to communicate the context of your messages and to make clear why your messages are relevant and important to them.

Taking Action: evaluate your most recent messages to your customers, such as brochures, advertising, and your website. Are you communicating just information and content? How can these messages be put into better context that is relevant to the recipients?

Are you still mass broadcasting your messages, using the spray and pray method in the hopes of attracting a wider audience?

How can you begin to narrowcast and personalize your messages to your key customers and other important constituents?

What communications channels can you open that will entice your key audiences to provide you with important feedback and the start of two-way, interactive dialogues?

Communications Trend #2

In the previous memo, we began to explore some of the significant trends impacting the ability of organizations to communicate to their key audiences effectively and efficiently today.

The second trend impacting the communications process is that a huge disintegration gap has developed between the marketing communications messages being sent by organizations and the receipt and comprehension of these messages by the marketplace.

There are five reasons for this communications gap, and they are:

1. The massive proliferation of products, services, and brand options available.

2. The focus of too many marketing communications messages on brand and product *names* rather than brand characteristics and persona. Such communications hope to generate name recognition and recall at the point of sale,

instead of developing and communicating unique brand characteristics.

3. A near universal acceptance that many product categories are now commodities in terms of product features, promotional activities, pricing, and distribution.

4. Higher levels of mistrust by the general public of both advertising and product claims.

5. Informed and demanding customers replacing the uniformed.

The fourth point — increased and widespread consumer mistrust in advertising and product claims — may the most worrisome for marketers. When surveys, such as the one conducted by Video Storyboard Tests, reveal that as many as 75% of respondents think all or some television advertising is unbelievable, marketers must stop and re-evaluate how and why they are still engaging in one-way, unconvincing forms of communications.

A third trend, greatly enhanced by modern technology, is that the individual has become the mass. This trend is just starting to evolve and develop, and we are certainly a long way from seeing it applied from pole to pole across all industries.

Customization and personalization have always been key differentiating factors in defining levels of customer service. Now, however, the trend toward customization of both product offer and service delivery is already having an impact in some manufacturing sectors.

Levi Strauss already offers customized jeans to be ordered, so customers no longer have to fit into jeans made to standard sizes. Dell Computer revolutionized the personal computer industry by allowing customers to order PCs to individual specifications and needs.

If you want an off-the-shelf computer, visit a retail outlet. If you want to have your own modified version with more memory, a different processing chip, a smaller or larger screen, or more USB ports, give a call to Dell— or visit their highly acclaimed website — and your new **personalized computer** (a major step up from it just being a *personal* computer) will be shipped to you within a few days or sooner.

Both of these trends — the growing disintegration between the messages communicated and the information received....and the movement toward treating the individual customer as the mass — are important factors in the way organizations will want to evolve their communications strategies for the future.

The bottom line is that it takes informed, motivated, and committed employees to achieve and maintain customer and business partner relationships. From a communications standpoint, the more well-informed the organization and customer become about each other, the greater is the chance of a mutually beneficial relationship being developed and sustained.

The more your audiences know about your organization, the more they understand its core values and appreciate its endeavors, the greater is the chance that they will identify with your organization.

This is one of the most elevated forms of bonding and attachment available for sustaining a desirable relationship with either customers or business partners.

A planned and well-managed corporate image is the most promising marketing prescription for conquering the current attitudes audiences have towards today's marketing communications problems.

There is no other marketing panacea as powerful as an organization that understands itself, knows where it is headed, and that relishes two-way communications with its key audiences.

Key Point: with all the noise in the market place, there is a huge disintegration gap between the marketing communications messages being sent by organizations and the receipt and comprehension of these messages.

Taking Action: how well do your customers understand your organization, your core values, and your endeavors? Do your customers have an identified link with your organization? Why or why not?

Where can the bonds be formed with your key customers so that a desirable and mutually rewarding relationship can be formed?

Are your employees well informed, motivated, and committed? If they are not well informed, how can they possibly be responsible for effectively communicating your values and commitments to your customers?

Communications Trend #3

We've been discussing in the last two essays some of the significant trends impacting the ability of organizations to communicate to their key audiences effectively and efficiently.

The last significant trend to mention is one that is evolving slowly and is weaving its way into the annals of marketing literature and practices.

This is the move from integrated *marketing communications* to integrated *marketing*.

As explained in their book *Driving Brand Value*, Tom Duncan and Sandra Moriarty describe the primary differences between their version of integrated marketing and traditional marketing as:

- Shifting the emphasis from acquiring customers to retaining and growing existing customer bases.

- Communicating *with,* rather than just *to,* customers and stakeholders.

- Expanding the marketing responsibility beyond the marketing department, making marketing less a function and more a philosophy of doing business.

On all three of these points, we whole-heartedly agree.

These authors place the integrated marketing concept squarely at both the product brand and the corporate brand levels. Thus, integrated marketing is used to drive relationships with customers and other stakeholders through marketing and communications efforts.

By comparison, in our book *Corporate Image Management: A Marketing Discipline for the 21st Century*, we advocate using the corporate image management process as a philosophy of doing business in order to develop relationships at the corporate brand level that are received through consistent experiences and interactions delivered by the organization.

The differences between our two approaches are not great. As a matter of fact, they are more complementary than opposing.

Theirs is a more outward looking perspective with integrated marketing strategies aimed at customers and other stakeholders.

Ours is both an outward and an inward approach, which takes into greater consideration the need for an organization to develop a unifying corporate culture and an agreed upon set of corporate behavior patterns that allow for the seamless execution of the desired corporate image.

With the corporate image management process, employees, business partners, and suppliers become equally important target audiences as customers, shareholders, and other so-called outside audiences.

Another thing we both agree on is that the integration of marketing communications tools and efforts will be to no avail if the organization is projecting more powerful and contradictory messages through its actions. In our opinion, such contrary messages not only make integrated marketing communications efforts fruitless, but they result in negative consequences for the organization as it gains a reputation for being (at best) inconsistent or (at worst) dishonest.

Everything your organization is currently doing is already communicating to each of your intended and unintended audiences. To ensure that the right messages are being communicated and received, the organization must put into place the most powerful marketing discipline available — the corporate image management process.

Because, at the end of the day....your competitors can mimic and better your product offer. They can create stronger distribution systems than yours. They can outspend you in advertising and promotions. And, of course, they can always beat you up on price.

But the one thing a competitor cannot mimic or copy is a well-defined corporate personality.

As I have written several times during the essays found in this book, my marketing philosophy is very simple — *if it touches the customer, it's a marketing issue.*™

And nothing, nothing touches the customer more than how he or she perceives your corporate image.

Key Point: it is time for most organizations to move from integrated marketing communications to integrated marketing.

Taking Action: think clearly about your communications processes — are you communicating *to* your customers or truly communicating *with* them?

How can you make marketing less a departmental function and more a philosophy and way of doing business for the entire organization?

Is there any disconnect between what your organization says about itself in its marketing communications materials and the messages communicated through its actions and interactions with customers? How can you do a better job of living up to the promises made in your marketing literature?

Using Outside Resources

The development of relationship excellence in any organization requires perpetual innovation and improvement. Often, the most effective way to introduce this kind of continuous improvement program is through the experience and expertise of outside resources.

Humans generally resist and resent change. This is unfortunate, for the very nature of business today is a world consumed by change. Sometimes this change will be evolutionary, sometimes revolutionary. Either way, it is merely a precursor to the future organizational state, in which change and flexibility will be constant requirements for organizations to adapt to the changing and evolving needs of customers.

Perhaps, when change becomes a more prevalent norm, and adaptability becomes a core competency for organizations, today's natural discomfort with change will cease or subside.

The role of the outside marketing consultant is to help the organization pass the various stages of change resistance, acceptance, and implementation so that relationship excellence can be infused as a new core competency.

To succeed in today's highly competitive markets, management must be willing to invest *now* in the necessary financial and human resources, and in the internal procedures and processes required to re-align the organization into a customer-centric concern. The window of opportunity for doing so closes ever so slightly with each passing day.

The most important value of an outside resource, particularly in the early stages of this re-alignment, is the advantage gained from an independent diagnosis of the organization's current market and image situation, and its future potential in both these areas.

Additionally, the early stages of the process require an enormous time commitment by a range of specialists and marketing practitioners, time that is unlikely to be available by appropriate people within the organization unless they are completely relieved of all other commitments, duties, and responsibilities.

The strategic marketing consultants will need to be empowered by management to conduct a thorough review and analysis of the organization, not simply a review of its relationship marketing procedures and practices. The wider the latitude given to the consultants, and the greater their access to information and key people (both internally and externally), the better will be the recommendations and strategies.

Empowerment, however, does not mean abandonment. Both the consultants and the client should view this process as an "arm-in-arm" program, in which the client remains actively engaged at all times. The only area of the process to exclude the client is research, in order to maintain the strictest levels of confidentiality and openness.

The second greatest benefit of using outside resources comes from the impartial and confidential role of the consultant. Impartiality allows objective appraisal and analysis of the information uncovered during the investigative stage. Confidentiality allows a wide range of unknown issues, beliefs, feelings, and concerns to be raised by all parties. Also, this ensures that everyone's "pet projects" are given equal hearing and evaluation.

Additionally, the use of outside consultants can often harness across-the-board commitment to the project.

Engaging an external consultant is often a key signal to the organization that the project is serious and that management is willing to admit that it does not have all the answers nor all the internal resources in place.

Also, external resources can often keep a project moving along, without it becoming delayed or bogged down by new priorities and day-to-day concerns.

Successful marketing has always been about correctly identifying or anticipating customer needs and fulfilling those needs. This will not change in the future. However, we are entering a world in which the deeper, emotional needs of relationship fulfilment become a predominant factor in the customer purchase decision-making process.

Getting to the stage where your organization is customer-centric or customer-focused is not always an easy endeavor. Sometimes, the most effective way to get there is through the experience and expertise of outside resources.

Key Point: outside resources can enable you to pass through the various stages of change resistance quicker, and with greater group buy-in.

Taking Action: how well does your organization respond to "moments of truth?" Is this response usually that of a product-driven or of a customer-focused organization?

What would it take to become customer-centric throughout the organization? Do you have the internal resources to see this through? What other "priorities" might crop up that could sideline this initiative while it is in progress?

Where will your future growth come from — new or existing customers? What relationship developing capabilities do you have in place for each of these customer segments?

Will an outside resource do a better job of creating organization-wide attention, spreading the gospel, and generating support for the change initiative? Why or why not?

Selecting Outside Resources

Having assisted several clients in the selection of external consultants, and having been on the pitching side of the business numerous times myself, it never ceases to amaze me how often the process of selection goes astray. And the problem usually results from one simple oversight — failing to agree on the selection criteria *before* the start of the presentation cycle.

There are few things more frustrating than having several teams of professional consultants make their pitches, and then have the evaluation panel spend precious time *afterwards* trying to determine which criteria to use in comparing the very different strategies and ideas presented. In the end, someone always suggests an arbitrary scorecard, a vote is taken, and the results are fairly split across all the candidates with no clear winner. The rankings are then rationalized, a group consensus forms, and the selection is usually the team that exhibited the closest chemistry to the evaluation panel (or more specifically to the head of the client team).

This is not to suggest that chemistry is not important, because it is. But it should not be the ultimate and final criterion unless it is used simply to break two closely ranked bids.

For what it's worth, here are five key items I recommend that my clients include on their scorecards *before* they start watching and listening to agency presentations:

1. Relevant experience — not necessarily within the same industry, but in successfully handling projects of similar size and nature.

2. Understanding needs — how well did the consultants understand the initial brief? Did they take the brief and respond to it, or did they also investigate the client's situation and add valuable points for consideration? Are they likely to react only to stated concerns, or will they help expand the client's horizon and thought processes, challenging them to think outside their existing belief boxes?

3. Integrity — a critical factor. The consultants are going to be exposed to vast amounts of company data and will

be privy to growth plans, business strategies, hiring practices, and other corporate secrets. If the consultants are too willing to share secrets or exchange rumors about the organizations they have worked with in the past, that is often a good sign that the client's own stories and gossip will be spread after the conclusion of the assignment.

4. Consulting team — the composition of the consulting team to be assigned to the account is the most critical factor to be evaluated. Specifics need to be understood and generalities (like "Bill worked on XYZ project) tested for details. It is important to also know how many times this team has worked together and on what business and types of projects.

5. Style and fit — lastly, the consultants should have some natural fit with the organization and its corporate culture. This should be with the bulk of the company, and not only with the "suits"

located in the executive offices. While some aspects of style and fit relate directly to chemistry, other details include communications style, documentation, dress, vocabulary, jargon, social interests, and demeanor.

Using a scorecard approach to compare the various consultants and their proposals allows the client evaluation panel to score each prospect with agreed upon criteria. This will help to make the final selection as unanimous as possible. If a near unanimous decision cannot be made by the evaluation panel, then this is probably a sign that the panel's members are not clear about their objectives or that they are not truly ready to undertake and proceed with a strategic initiative program.

Key Point: it is important to decide *before* the presentations begin what criteria will be used for the selection of outside consultants.

Taking Action: what are your expectations of the deliverables that the outside resources will deliver during and at the conclusion of a project?

Who is most likely to play an active role, from your organization, in the project? Identify this person's key concerns, desires, and wish list *before* the short list of candidates are briefed. Include appropriate items in the brief.

What special considerations or unusual circumstances might crop up during the length of the project and how would these impact the project?

Changing Customer Values

The many forces reshaping the world economy today are more numerous, more interwoven, and combine to be more powerful than any other combination of economic and political change since the Industrial Revolution.

Change is happening so rapidly that the countless reorganizations, restructurings, downsizings, mergers, break-ups, and new business start-ups make the business community seem almost out of control.

It is not at all surprising, therefore, that your customers are undergoing vast amounts of change.

Customers will continue to present a vast array of challenges and opportunities. However, these challenges and opportunities are unlikely to be as apparent and as stationary as in the past. Understanding customers in the future will definitely require hitting a moving target!

I see seven key areas where customers are most likely to focus their value judgements in the future:

1. Relevant features and functions and ability to customize solutions

2. Choices and Flexibility

3. Relationships based on trust and rewarded with loyalty

4. Sufficient knowledge and information

5. Complete and full satisfaction

6. Speed and convenience

7. Environmental impact

Customer-centric organizations will need to use an understanding of these changing customer values to create the most successful and dynamic businesses of the future. These evolving customer values will drive customer expectations in the future, and hence will determine which products and services succeed in the market place.

In the past, organizations only had to worry about being the best, within their particular niche, within whatever geographic territory they decided to conduct business. This is no longer the case.

Your competitors no longer live down the street or across town. They're just as likely to be found halfway around the globe. Even if the competitor is not fighting you for the same clients (e.g. customers of a local bank are not likely to be pursued by a multinational bank eight time zones away), it may very well be fighting you for the same capital and human resources, the same raw materials, or the same distribution channels.

And, with the growth of the Internet as a sales distribution channel, combined with the lowering of import tariffs around the world, your competition for sales may well indeed reside outside your geographic market place. If the product or service can be sourced from remote suppliers and delivered by a third party, the Internet removes all barriers and borders to where your competitors can be found.

For instance, already today I can live in one country and have my banking facilities, book store, music store, news and information sources, software suppliers, and much more all located outside my country of residence. And this is just the start.

As long as these "external" suppliers can meet my personal customer value concerns, they are just as likely to get my business as a supplier who is located nearer to me.

Obviously, these seven value judgment categories will not apply equally to all. Also, it can be anticipated that individual customers will use different value judgements for different product and service categories.

However, these seven areas are likely to cause the most dramatic shifts in customer buying behavior and habits. As a result, they are also likely to have the most dramatic impact on forward-looking organizations as these adapt their product offers and service delivery processes to meet these changing requirements.

The key, as always, is understanding which of the customer values are most important to each specific customer, and then providing fully satisfying solutions to those customers whose needs your organization can meet profitably.

Key Point: what customers value will continue to evolve, resulting in changing customer expectations for both products and services.

Taking Action: how have your customer expectations changed in the past 2-3 years? How are they likely to change in the next couple of years?

Do you see a correlation between changing customer expectations and changing customer values? What impact will this have on your business as these customer values continue to change?

Which of these seven changing customer values are most applicable to your industry, products, and services? How can you position your products and services to get ahead of this change curve?

Changing Customer Values: Relevant Functions and Features and Ability to Customize Solutions

The old school of manufacturing and marketing was to pack as many features and functions into the product and then let the customer choose which ones they want to use.

This strategy will no longer win you loyal customers, particularly with the astute customers we see today.

Rather, implementation of flexible manufacturing techniques and allowing for customization at the ordering stage is the best strategy to meet changing customer requirements. Effectively the order placement stage becomes the ordering *and design* stage.

And, since customers are willing to wait for their self-created, personalized products to arrive, such flexible manufacturing reduces the need for product and finished goods inventory throughout the sales distribution channels.

Customers want to have more say in which features and functions are loaded onto their products. An example where this first took place is in the personal computer industry. Dell Computers created an entire new business model by giving customers the opportunity to select which features and functions to be put into their computers.

In doing so, Dell changed the concept of these machines from personal computers to *personalized* computers, and changed the industry in doing so. Several other computer manufacturers and assemblers have followed in Dell's footsteps, either fully or partially.

It won't be long until the same flexible customized manufacturing process is applied to many other industries.

This is not to say that customers will no longer be price or cost conscious. Rather, I would project that the customers are becoming extremely "value conscious," in that they will seek the best value-for-money option made available to them.

I am not saying that manufacturers should strip down their products to the bare essentials. I disagree with those who advocate eliminating all unnecessary features in one's products and services and focusing only on the value-adding or enhancing attributes that customers want or expect. That's exactly where we are today, for one person's wants or expectations are another person's unwanted product features.

The benefit to marketers of this particular changing customer value yardstick is, for those who get the manufacturing equation right, higher margins and higher profitability. After all, if you are delivering value, and above all *personalized* value, then you have the opportunity to be charging at value pricing rates.

When the customer is willing to exchange money for value, then you have a distinct advantage over the traditional techniques of cost-plus pricing, market entry pricing, commodity pricing, discount pricing, and even market premium pricing.

Delivering value for money. Sounds like a sensible business model to me.

Key Point: customers place high value on the ability to incorporate relevant features and functions into the products they buy and use.

Taking Action: where are the opportunities in your product line to offer customers the selection of the features and functions built into your products?

How can you make the delivery of optional features and functions available to customers through remote delivery channels such as the Internet?

Are your products packed with functions and features that customers rarely use and/or do not value? What savings could be found if you eliminated these? How could these be delivered only to those who do value them?

Changing Customer Values:
Choices and Flexibility

Customers continue to place a high value on choices and flexibility.

We are seeing this trend already today, as an increasing number of products are marketed like Swatch watches — in a multitude of styles, models, colors, and interchangeable options. Even the Apple iMac computer attracted buyers just as much for its fashionable designs and color options as for its computer prowess and chip speeds.

Your customers are likely to expect a wide array of choices and variety in the products you market. However, many managers and marketers fail to understand that variety is not the same thing as customization. Offering a variety of options is one strategy. However, as we discussed in the previous *Powerful Marketing* Memo, providing customization is entirely different.

Some industries simply do not lend themselves to customization (of the product). For instance, in the airline industry one cannot expect to have the plane customized to one's personal taste, or for the route to be altered to accommodate one's particular needs.

However, the airlines have certainly learned how to provide variety in their product offers — knowing full well that some passengers will pay extra for the comfort and prestige of flying in Business Class or First Class, while others are simply interested in being moved from point A to point B as efficiently and safely as possible.

Other choices the airlines provide include time of travel, non-stop and indirect routes, onboard amenities and entertainment, and the types of aircraft flown.

Note, however, that all industries can customize their services. As such the individual *customer experience* with every product and industry can be customized.

In terms of flexibility, customers already place a high value on organizations that have flexible policies and procedures. One of the most hated phrases customers hear is *it's our policy*. That simply tells the customer that you are not recognizing him or her as an individual with individual needs. Rather, the organization is saying that the customer is no different from any other customer and hence must conform to the organization's stated policy.

Companies that can train and empower their people, particularly their frontline people, in interpreting and applying corporate policies as guidelines will in turn generate higher levels of loyalty and repeat business from customers.

Policies that concern corporate ethics and that could have *major* impact on profitability should certainly be followed to the letter. However, policies that have to do with internal procedures and processes, and which have direct impact on the organization's ability to meet customer needs, should be used as guidelines to help employees deal with specific customer situations.

If you cannot build the flexible manufacturing capabilities required for customization, then your next best alternative is to produce a wide variety of product offers and options for customers. In either case, to attract future customers you will need to have flexible policies and procedures in place.

Key Point: customers today, and in the future, value choices, options and, most of all, flexible corporate policies.

Taking Action: how many product options do you currently offer? Might there be a need for more, or fewer? How can you determine this without risking negative customer publicity?

How flexible are your policies? Would your frontline staff encourage more flexibility? Would your customers appreciate more flexibility? How can you change your current procedures and processes to make them more flexible?

Assuming that your products cannot be customized, how might your service delivery be customized? What benefits would you derive from this?

Changing Customer Values:
Trust and Loyalty

Is there a lack of trust by customers, particularly consumers, in business today?

Admittedly, the answer is yes.

The combined effect of product-tampering problems, toxic-shock syndrome, the Perrier recall, mad cow disease, hepatitis-infected fruit given to school children, the health scare in Belgium when children got sick from drinking Coca-Cola, and numerous other safety scares has left consumers in a quandary about who and what to trust.

Will customers really reward trust with loyalty? I believe they will.

Loyalty, however, cannot be bought. It has to be won. It has to be earned. True loyalty will not result from reward schemes and customer loyalty point schemes.

Customers are kept loyal through consistency in the level of product quality, brand characteristics, and service excellence received each time a purchase is made and each time a product is used or consumed.

Consistent delivery of these three attributes builds trust. Consistent receipt of these three attributes leads to repeat purchases, which in turn leads to brand, product, and corporate loyalty.

Customers place a higher value on the brands and companies they trust.

Interestingly, during times of economic down turns, consumers tend to turn to the brands and products they know best (and trust most), rather than to the low-priced generic alternatives.

This says a lot about human nature and, based on Maslow's Hierarchy of Needs, makes perfect sense. Customers need to satisfy their need for security well before their need for socialization or esteem. Choosing the well-known and most trusted product is certainly motivated by safety and security concerns, as the risk of making the wrong choice when one has limited money is much greater than when one has ample funds.

Why do I believe that trust will be rewarded with loyalty? Because it's usually in the customer's best interest!

After all, for the customer, trust:

- Shortens and simplifies the buying decision process.

- Creates rational and emotional criteria for repeat purchases.

- Creates rational and emotional criteria for product and brand loyalty.

In other words, trust not only simplifies the buying decision process, it also saves the customer time and mental aggravation over having to make a decision. And the one thing we all say we're short of is time! Anything that can save the customer time and anguish are sure to be seen by the customer as highly valued benefits.

For the marketer, building trust with customers has the key benefit of also helping to prevent customer attrition.

Consistent delivery of product quality, brand characteristics, and service excellence are the best ways to develop trust. Add to this complete satisfaction of the customer's needs, and you develop a situation where the customer has no reason to even think of going anywhere else.

As stated elsewhere in *Powerful Marketing Memos*, it is really a simple equation:

> A commitment to quality and consistent delivery leads to complete satisfaction.

> Complete satisfaction leads to repeat purchases.

> Repeat purchases lead to customer loyalty.

Building the future of your business on trust. Being rewarded with customer loyalty. Once again, it sounds like a good business model to me.

Key Point: customers place a high value on trust, particularly when such trust saves them time and mental anguish.

Taking Action: how trustworthy is your organization? Now, ask it again, how *truly* trustworthy is your organization — in terms of consistent quality and service delivery?

Do your customers view you as a trusted partner? Do your customers view your organization as reliable? Why or why not?

How can the perception of your organization as trusted and reliable be improved? How can this perception be improved through the organization's behavior patterns?

Changing Customer Values:
Knowledge and Information

Customers today are highly knowledgeable, even more so than only a few years ago. And, they are used to making purchase decisions after having done thorough research and investigations into the multitude of options available.

As a result, they place a high value on organizations and products that provide them with full, or at least sufficient, knowledge and information while they are in the research phase of the buying process.

Will the access to information make customers even more price sensitive, and price knowledgeable, than they are today? Undoubtedly yes, at least to an extent.

However, as it is today, price is not always the key or final determinant in the purchase decision. Some customers, of course, only buy on price. But those tend to be your lowest margin customers anyway. So unless you're in a massively high-volume business, low-margin customers are not the best thing to have anyway.

More important, however, the access to instant information now results in global standards (particularly for quality) and in global attitudes towards functions, features, choices, options, and flexibility. Those who can meet these customer requirements on a global basis will surpass by far those dealing in parity products selling at less than optimal prices.

In addition, by providing global access to information and product specifications, and using third-party shippers to deliver their products, organizations are able to market their products on a worldwide basis without having to establish intricate distribution channels in countless countries and territories.

It also means that such companies do not have to share their margins with several tiers of distribution channels, thus capturing larger margins for themselves, even when forced to discount their prices to customers.

Understanding this need of customers for ready access to information, organizations must adapt their customer support operations accordingly. Being open only during the so-called "business hours" no longer applies. Business in the Internet Age is 24x7, public holidays included.

As a result, organizations have to look to outsource customer service and customer enquiry operations into low-cost labor markets through the use of technology. The advantage, of course, is that many of these low-cost labor markets are in parts of the world several time zones away from the developed markets, and hence it will be easier to procure staff to work outside the normal daylight business hours of the home market.

There is little doubt that the access to, and the desire for, up-to-date information will result in greater switching by customers. After all, one big advantage of the Internet for customers is the greatly reduced switching costs it provides.

However, customers will only switch if their current product or service provider is not meeting their requirements on their highest values and most important criteria. Again, if customers are fully satisfied, why would they look elsewhere?

The key, as always, is understanding which of the customer values are most important to each specific customer, and then providing fully satisfying solutions to those customers whose needs your organization can meet profitably.

Let's see....meeting customer needs profitably. Once again, this sounds like a good business model to me.

Key Point: customers place a high value on obtaining sufficient knowledge and information that helps their own decision-making processes.

Taking Action: compare yourself to your major competitors in the amount, quality, and relevancy of the information you each provide to customers. Which one of you makes access to information easiest for customers?

How can you increase the accessibility to information for your customers?

Can you turn the provision of information, particularly industry-related information, into a value-added service that will be appreciated and valued by your customers?

Changing Customer Values:
Complete and Full Satisfaction

Customers have one all-important characteristic in common — the desire for the products and services they purchase, and use, to deliver complete and full satisfaction.

For this reason, it is easy to appreciate that customers place a high value, perhaps the highest value, on products, services, and organizations that consistently deliver complete and full satisfaction.

It is the total experience with the product or service that counts — beginning with the search for information right through to usage, disposal, or return. That is right, in an increasingly environmentally conscious world, how your product is disposed of will become of greater importance.

As I have said and written before, customers want full satisfaction, not merely customer delight or customer service that "knocks their socks off." Quite frankly, I think most customers would prefer to keep their socks on!

If you will recall one of my customer-focused marketing maxims is: *customers do not buy products, they buy solutions.* This maxim will apply with even greater intensity in the future, as knowledgeable customers seek to understand the wide range of options available to them before making a purchase decision. As not all possible solutions are likely to come from the same product field or industry, your competition in the future is likely to come from further afield than ever before.

Additionally, as the world economies continue to strengthen and a larger portion of the earth's population moves into the middle and upper socio-economic tiers, products and services of the future will need to satisfy more than just the basic needs and wants of customers. Your products will need to move up Maslow's Hierarchy of Needs scale to encompass the social, esteem, and self-actualization needs of your customers.

Likewise, products and services that appeal to several senses will do better than those that appeal to only one or two. Note how the Apple iMac changed the computer industry overnight just by adding a splash of color to our previously monotone desktop PCs.

(And why hadn't anyone thought or implemented this rather fundamental total customer experience before?) Many of you will soon be selling "experiences," not just products or services!

Also, organizations that can integrate various components and services, and take responsibility for their interoperability, will be greatly rewarded. Again, the PC industry took a step in this direction by pre-loading operating software and even application software onto our computers before we brought them home. Unfortunately, few seemed to take responsibility when users had problems with the software.

There is a great opportunity awaiting anyone who can move from providing solitary products and partial solutions to providing fully integrated solutions. I know this particular customer truly values the organizations that integrate separate components into one solution. However, I would value even more greatly the organizations who monitored my situation and could advise me on when it is time to upgrade or add on additional components. Now that would be a fully satisfying experience!

Again, I cannot overemphasize the fact that fully satisfying experiences will be rewarded with repeat purchases and long-term loyalty.

Hmm....building the future of your business on repeat purchases and long-term loyalty. Makes sense to me.

Key Point: customers reward complete and full satisfaction with repeat purchases and loyalty.

Taking Action: what would it take to achieve complete and full satisfaction with your key (top 20%) customers?

What opportunities are there for you to provide value-added services by integrating other products or services that customers use when they buy or use your products or services?

Describe the "total experience" customers have with your product or service, from the search for information stage right through to use or consumption. Where are the weak links? Where are your strengths? How can you improve the weak links? How can you leverage and/or further improve your strengths?

Changing Customer Values:
Speed and Convenience

There are three key areas concerning speed and convenience that customers value the most:

- ◆ Shorter product cycles.

- ◆ Shorter order lead times and faster delivery times.

- ◆ Smaller quantities per order.

It might seem like shorter product cycles would be a negative for customers, but I don't think it will be for most. The key advantage for customers of shorter product cycles is that putting off a buying decision becomes less painful. There's no need to order the latest mobile phone, or the latest notebook computer, today when we all know that: a) a newer model will be available within months, and b) the price of today's model is most likely to drop when the next new model appears.

On the other hand, no one likes to feel that he or she owns an obsolete product. But with the speed of technological advances these days, everyone knows that they are only going to be at the razor's edge of the product curve for a very short time.

Additionally, for those who can afford it, shorter product life cycles, combined with lower out-of-pocket costs, make it easier to upgrade to the latest model.

As a result, it is now no big deal for some people to buy a new mobile phone every year or so.

However, this is not to hint or infer that the customers will accept shorter life cycles due to poor product quality or short durability. We can actually expect just the opposite to happen — customers require, demand actually, high quality and durability of products lasting well beyond their initial ownership periods.

Interestingly, as consumers get used to replacing and upgrading mobile phones, desktop computers, notebooks, and other products, one wonders if they will also start to replace home appliances, televisions, car stereos, and other items on a more frequent basis?

Both industrial customers and consumers place increasing value on shorter lead times and faster delivery times. For consumers, the ability to shop on the Internet and know that delivery will take place with days is fast becoming an expectation. Woe be it to the organization that finds itself short of inventory for its online customers.

Just a few years ago, holding inventory was perceived to be an important part of the value chain. Now, it's considered a financial liability and no one wants to take a risk of having too much inventory. However, in today's world, not having sufficient inventory is likely to be even riskier than having too much — for once a customer moves on to another supplier who does have the desired inventory in stock, you are not likely to woo this customer back for some time.

Likewise, industrial customers are apt to order in smaller lot sizes, with frequent orders replacing large ones. It is now a world of just-in-time deliveries and customers are placing a high value on the supplier who can consistently and reliably meet their needs for JIT delivery without being early or late.

Customers want speed, convenience, quality, and reliability. Pretty demanding aren't they? But then again, aren't you just as demanding whenever you are the customer?

Key Point: customers place extremely high value on speed, convenience, and your ability to deliver when and where they want.

Taking Action: what are the three things you do best in terms of speed and convenience for your customers? How can you leverage these into higher value propositions for your customers?

What are the three things you do worst in terms of speed and convenience for your customers? How quickly can these items be rectified?

Is your business model built on manufacturing high volume quantities? Do you see the trend towards smaller and more frequent orders? What processes need to be changed so that you can remain profitable in this new world?

Changing Customer Values: Environmental Impact

No one knows for sure how environmentally conscious and supportive customers are likely to be in the future. However, one will not be far wrong if one supposes that environmental concerns will be *no less important* in the future than they are today.

And, in fact, it is very likely that concern for the environment will become *even more important* for an increasing number of customers. Why?

Well, for one thing, several government initiatives, mostly in North America and Europe, are leading the way. Europe, for instance, has specific rules and regulations now regarding packaging materials and the need for these to be biodegradable. In California, the state government enforces some of the strictest rules in the country concerning automobile emissions. Even India has followed suit and is adopting European standards for vehicle emissions.

The environmental movement is one area that organizations seem keen to associate with these days. However, environmentally conscious consumers are well aware that, except for a handful of truly exceptional cases, most of these efforts are mere tactical promotions and many are more self-serving than environmentally serving.

However, for companies that do want to truly benefit from the environmental movement, there will be a core constituency available who will highly value the use of environmentally friendly materials and processes in the manufacturing and distribution of products.

These opportunities run the gamut from the use of recycled raw materials to incorporating materials, parts, ingredients, and packaging that are biodegradable into your final products.

Even service companies can jump on the environmental bandwagon. For instance, the HongkongBank *Care for Nature* MasterCard is an affinity program in Malaysia and Singapore that allows cardholders to associate themselves with support for nature.

In this program, a small percentage of each cardholder transaction goes into a special trust fund, managed by HongkongBank, which is used to fund special environmental activities in these two countries. This program, and others like it around the world, has been very successful in creating awareness for environment concerns and in delivering a highly valued affinity credit card product to environmentally conscious and active consumers.

While the environmentally conscious consumer is not yet a large mass-market opportunity, these folks do tend to be very adamant and very loyal in their support of environment issues. Hence, they have the capacity to become your friend or your foe.

Thus, if there's an opportunity for your organization to be truly involved and supportive of the environment and the environmental movement, not only will we all benefit (from cleaner air, reduced use of fossil fuels, etc.), but you are likely to develop a core nucleus of dedicated and loyal customers.

Let's see — helping the environment while also simultaneously creating a loyal and dedicated customer base. It is probably not a bad business model for all of us to consider.

Key Point: an increasing number of your customers will place a high value on your support for the environment and environmental issues.

Taking Action: how can you truly help the environmental movement and, at the same time, capitalize on your involvement?

Is there an affinity group of environmentally conscious customers who would appreciate, and reward your organization, for deeper involvement, and/or conspicuous concern for the environment?

What have you got to lose by being concerned about the environment? What have you got to gain?

Creating Complete Customer Satisfaction

I often advise senior management and business owners that their companies and organizations today need to change from a focus on trying to win new customers to concentrating on meeting and satisfying the needs of their current customer bases.

With this strategy, the aim is to achieve a high degree of **complete customer satisfaction** with the customers you already have in hand.

Good customer service is no longer good enough. As a matter of fact, I encourage each of you reading this *Powerful Marketing Memo* today to "fire" all of your customer service staff. That's right, *fire them*. And then hire them back 15 minutes later as **customer satisfaction** staff.

I am not playing a game of semantics with you. Customer service tends to be reactionary and process oriented. Customer service people are often measured on how many customer complaints they handle per shift.

Customer satisfaction is both more anticipatory and pro-active. First, it seeks to ensure that the customer is fully satisfied, not merely mollified with a quick-fix solution or an apologetic reward.

Second, customer satisfaction is also a mindset that seeks to anticipate future customer needs and therefore prevents the organization from making future mistakes and errors.

Numerous research studies have shown that if you can reduce your attrition rate....that is the annualized rate of lost customers....by as little as five percentage points, you can increase your bottom-line profits by anywhere from 25% to 85%!

That's right, just keeping more of the customers you have, and preventing them from taking their business elsewhere, can have an immediate positive impact on your profits.

The single best way to keep customers from leaving? Completely satisfy their needs!

Then they will have no need to look elsewhere for solutions to their problems or opportunities.

Key Point: you can increase your bottom-line profits by as much as 85% just by reducing customer attrition.

Taking Action: what would it take to change the mindset of your customer service people so that they became more pro-active and thought of themselves as customer satisfaction people?

What would it take to change the mindset of your management team so that they knew how to manage, motivate, and reward a customer satisfaction staff?

Sales/Service Relationship

Many organizations segment their service function from their sales activities. I believe this is a mistake.

The closer you can entwine your service and sales activities, the more successful you are likely to be. After all, the customer rarely segments a sales activity from a service activity. To him or her, *all* your activities are service related!

The formula for weaving these two activities together is to:

- ◆ Turn service opportunities into sales opportunities.

- ◆ Use sales opportunities to provide efficient and appreciated service.

Another way of expressing this is: SALES = SERVICE = SUCCESS.

Some people like to argue that this expression should read "sales + service = success." But that is where I disagree. That is the way of doing things today, with sales being one activity and service being another.

Changing your mindset to SALES = SERVICE = SUCCESS means you understand that success comes when there's no segmentation between selling and service.

In today's age of consultative selling, one of the best services your organization can provide is to sell a customer the right product at the right time that provides the right solution for his or her particular need. Now that is a true service. One that every customer is likely to appreciate.

People often ask me: "How do you know if a customer is satisfied?"

The simple, and best, answer is, "ask." Be proactive. Call and ask the customer:

> "Did everything go as expected?"

> "Have we delivered as promised?"

> "Have we met your expectations?"

Staff should be encouraged to never be afraid of having to deal with problems. What if you do call up and there is a problem? Well, at least you are now aware of it, and you have an opportunity to fix the immediate problem — before it grows into something larger and more difficult to manage and rectify.

And by doing so, you not only show the customer that you *care* about them, but that you are also willing to *make sure* that they are completely satisfied — two concerns of customers that they will value highly.

Also, not following up always results in a missed selling opportunity.

When is the best time to start the next sales cycle? Any time the customer is fully satisfied with you. So, if nothing has gone wrong and the customer is completely satisfied, that's the ideal time to start working toward the next repeat order.

Or, once you've corrected any problems and have completely achieved customer satisfaction through your servicing efforts, you're in an ideal position to start working toward the next sale.

The Golden Rule of selling: *keep the customer completely satisfied, not just sold.*

Remember the earlier equation:

Quality results in customer satisfaction.

Customer satisfaction results in repeat buys.

Repeat purchases lead to customer loyalty.

By weaving together your sales and service mindsets, and being proactive in your customer care efforts, you will achieve the customer loyalty levels you are seeking.

Marketing is not rocket science. In fact, marketing success really boils down to two key principles: understanding customer needs and delivering upon the promises the organization makes. You can achieve these two principles through a full understanding and implementation of the sales/service relationship.

Key Point: it is important to weave together your sales and service activities so that they appear seamless to the customer.

Taking Action: are your sales people capable of superior service? Are your service people capable of superior selling? How can you fix any gaps that exist?

How can you make your staff more proactive in their customer care activities?

How can you inculcate the mantra SALES = SERVICE = SUCCESS throughout the organization?

What steps can you implement to keep your VIP customers completely satisfied, not just sold?

Making Life Inconvenient for Customers

Convenience is one of the 7 Cs of superior customer service. But sometimes I have to wonder, are organizations in the business of making things more convenient for their customers or for their staffs?

This question was highlighted to me late last year on a flight between Singapore and Melbourne. I was traveling on the airline that had made a reputation, right from its creation, as one delivering extraordinary customer service experiences to its passengers. However, on this flight, right outside the toilet door of a brand new aircraft was a sign that read, "Please give priority to crew members."

What?

Passengers should give priority to crew members when it comes to using the toilet? (Even more surprising, this was on the toilet door located in the First Class section.)

I asked one of the airline stewardesses for an explanation. "Well, we crew members have the need to go to the toilet too, you know?" she said, attempting to make a joke of her reply.

"Yes, I understand that," I replied in all seriousness. "But aren't your passengers your customers, and hence they should be given priority?"

She had no reply for this, and neither did her senior in-flight supervisor, when I overheard her ask him the same question. As the senior staff member on board, he should have approached me to see if this was a major concern of mine, or merely an inquisitive quandary. Rather, he chose to ignore me for the remaining five hours of the flight.

I was reminded of this situation when attempting to have a late breakfast this past weekend. I stopped by a nice looking restaurant at 11:10 on Saturday morning, deciding to enjoy the beautiful Melbourne summer weather for an al fresco breakfast. The waitress who approached took our coffee order and then proceeded to say, "We stopped serving breakfast at 11 and our lunch service starts at 11:30."

What?

"Does that mean you do not have any food service between 11:00 and 11:30?" I asked.

"Yes," she replied. "It gives the cooks time to clean the grills and prepare the ingredients for the lunch menu."

"I see," I thought. Here's a restaurant that understands it is more important to make things more convenient for its kitchen staff than for its customers.

So, for the next twenty minutes all we were able to order were liquid beverages. Not yet hungry for lunch, I moved on.

Of course, customer inconvenience doesn't only happen in service establishments like airlines and restaurants.

Unfortunately, it occurs way too often in a plethora of companies and organizations across a wide range of industries. Ones that readily come to my mind are:

- Banks, hotels, car rental companies, and other organizations that require customers to fill in forms with details such as address and telephone numbers, when they already have these details on file. Why can't these organizations protect a few trees, and save customers much valued time, by eliminating unnecessary paperwork?

- Magazines that ask customers to fill in address details on their websites when a customer is **renewing** a subscription. After all, if the magazine is currently being delivered to the correct address, and a customer wants to renew delivery at that address, why must the information be re-keyed in (and risk an entry error)?

- Doctors, dentists, physios and other medical practitioners who require patients (i.e. customers) to make appointments, and then let these patients sit in over-crowded, uncomfortable waiting rooms to be served 20-30 minutes after the appointed time. This really annoys me when my appointment is early in the morning, and the doctor is already running late before the first hour of the day is complete. When are patients going to start being treated like customers?

- Companies that cannot commit to a two-hour or three-hour delivery window, thus requiring the customer to "be there" all day waiting for delivery of goods already purchased. Why should a customer have to block off an entire day to wait for the delivery team?

- Customer service officers who promise to call back when a query or problem cannot immediately be handled on the phone, and then do not! Why make customers wait and wait and wait, and wonder and wonder what is happening?

- Organizations who require customers to call back to find out how a problem has been resolved, instead of being proactive and contacting the customer via phone, text message, fax, or email immediately when the resolution is determined. Why make the customer call you back?

In each of these instances, it might require a bit more work or effort on the part of the staff to prevent such inconveniences to customers. And yes, it would also require a bit more efficiency within the organization, as well as a more pro-active communications procedure with customers.

However, customers are the reason for your business (*raison d'etre*). Not your staff. Not your shareholders. As such, shouldn't your systems, processes, and procedures be geared towards greater convenience for your customers?

One of my favorite phrases is "life is too short to drink bad wine." I think we can paraphrase that for the world of marketing as "life is too short for us to cause wasted time and inconveniences for our customers."

For those organizations that take this message to heart and act upon it, you will be making one giant stride toward retaining your good customers and attracting equally as good ones through positive word of mouth.

Key Point: your systems, processes, and procedures should be geared toward providing greater convenience for your customers.

Taking Action: conduct an audit, or a mystery shopper, of the experiences customers have with your organization. Where can unnecessary paperwork be eliminated? Where can unnecessary waits by customers be avoided, eliminated, or reduced?

What are the situations that require customers to call back to your organization to find out how a situation or problem is being rectified? What would be required to change this to a pro-active system where your customers are called as soon as the resolution is determined, thus eliminating call backs by customers?

Ask your staff to start compiling a list of all customer comments, particularly negative statements, regarding inconvenience. Analyze this list for trends, or for new value-added services that you can start to offer.

Analyze your operating hour times, your delivery schedule times, and your telephone center times. What could be done to extend your operating times? What could be done to establish more specified delivery times to customers?

Delivering Upon Your Promises

Vernon Hill, President and CEO of Commerce Bank, is quoted in one of Fast Company's First Impression Newsletters as saying, "We have to keep delivering what we promise to customers."

When I first read this, I thought "how utterly silly" that a CEO of a major bank is making this kind of a statement. Is it really necessary to go all the way back to the very premise of what customer-focused marketing should be: identifying and serving the needs of customers by delivering upon our promises?

Upon the initial reading, the comment seemed almost trite. Or pithy, at best.

Then I started to recall a handful of incidents that had happened to this customer — all within the past month:

- The ticketing agent at one of my favorite airlines gave me wrong information about how I can use my frequent flier credits to upgrade on a flight the following week, resulting in one very unhappy customer at the airport a few days later when I tried to facilitate an upgrade.

- My phone company changed my billing address for *all* my accounts when I had new phone lines installed in a new premise, when all I wanted was for only the new phone lines to go onto a new account at the new address.

- The purchase of a new desktop computer from a world-famous computer company failed to arrive on the day specified, resulting in lost production, a highly distressed customer, and over 90 minutes wasted trying to get through the company's so-called help line.

- An order for a subscription to a major daily newspaper placed through the paper's Internet web site was miscommunicated to the newsagent assigned to deliver the paper, resulting in an order for the weekend edition being delivered instead of the daily edition.

And thus it began to occur to me that perhaps it is time for many organizations — particularly the four above — to return to the very basics of marketing and to re-focus internal efforts and energy on delivering upon their promises to customers.

There seems to be way too much focus today on price promotions, discounts, and channel incentives and not enough emphasis on solving customer needs and delivering upon the promises made to customers.

The fact is, no matter how much you reduce your selling price, lower margins, or engage in other short-term promotional programs, the customer still expects you to deliver upon your product, service, and organizational promises. This is just as true in B2B marketing, perhaps even more so, as in consumer marketing.

As Professor Craig Vogel of Carnegie Mellon University says in another Fast Company First Impression newsletter, "What people value and the way that they interact with a product goes beyond price."

The most fundamental way that customers interact with your organization, and your products and services, is through the promises made to them. These promises set their expectations. When their expectations are not met, especially basic and reasonable expectations, then such interactions have a huge negative impact on their relationship with your organization.

After all, as in the illustrations above, there is nothing unreasonable for a customer to expect:

- Factual information to be given.

- The billing address from the telephone service provider to be correct.

- Deliveries to be made on time and on the day specified.

- An order entered via a website to be communicated clearly and error-free to the distribution channel.

When I worked at Citibank in Singapore in the early 1990s, our retail bank service platform was based on the acronym CPT, which stood for Competence, Problem-Free, Timely.

At a minimum, today's customers expect you to deliver on all three of these values: having competent, knowledgeable staff, deliver problem-free products and services, and ensure delivery of your services and products in a timely fashion.

When you make a promise to a customer, be sure that your delivery upon each and every promise is competent, problem-free, and timely.

Keep (or start) delivering upon your promises to customers.

All else is secondary.

Key Point: you need to deliver upon the promises you make to customers.

Taking Action: start tracking all promises made to customers and monitor the time-frame for when actual delivery of these promises takes place. How often is your organization meeting promises within the specified time commitment? What steps are needed to improve this performance?

Where do frequent errors occur in your processes? What steps can be implemented to reduce or eliminate these errors?

If you outsource the physical delivery of your products, how do you monitor the performance of your service provider?

How long is the average wait time for customers calling into your call center? Making an upset customer wait an inordinate amount of time merely turns them into angry (or angrier) customers. What can be done to reduce time customers spend on hold?

Complaints Are Good

As sure as there are customers for your product, you can be guaranteed that there will be complaints about your products and services.

Why?

Is it impossible for an organization to deliver 100% customer satisfaction and 100% fault-free products and services all the time? In a simple word: yes.

I have yet to come across an organization that doesn't make the occasional mistake, or the employee who doesn't commit the odd accidental error or who simply is in a grumpy mood that is reflected onto your customers.

So face it — complaints will happen.

And this is good. For complaints are good for you.

One of the worst things customers can do when faced with unsatisfactory service or a poor quality product is to **not tell you and leave for the competition.** After all, if you don't hear of the problems that cause customers to take their business elsewhere, how can you fix them?

Customer complaints are good for these:

- Highlight areas that need improvement.

- Identify procedures that cause customer pain.

- Reveal information that is lacking, or erroneous, in your communications.

- Identify staff who need more training or closer supervision.

- Provide a check on consistency levels.

- Surface policies that may be outdated.

- Trigger positive change (if you take the initiative to act on the complaints).

- Raise staff morale (through positive change).

- Provide a method of competitive intelligence.

- Provide bench marking from other industries.

- Identify customers who care.

165

That last point is a critical one to ponder. ***Customers who complain are customers who care!***

Sure, customers who complain often want some form of restitution for the inconveniences suffered. But most just want the organization to live up to the promises made, which ought to be the key objective of the selling organization anyway.

So while they care about themselves and having their own satisfaction levels fulfilled, they also care enough about future engagements with the organization to want to help the organization live up to its commitments and prevent future service delivery or product problems.

Otherwise, they would simply just walk away and take their business elsewhere (after demanding a refund of whatever money has already been spent on the unsatisfactory product or service).

Whether they are loyal customers, upset customers, wronged customers, disappointed customers, angry customers, right customers, or even wrong customers — customers who complain do care. (Okay, maybe not all, but certainly most.)

If your staff attitudes can be shifted so that they collectively and individually view complainers as customers who care, then your organization is in a much better position to learn from such complaints and to implement restorative steps that result in retrieval of departing and departed customers.

Unfortunately, too many organizations treat customer complaints as "sore points" that need to be counted, rectified, and forgotten as soon as the service staff moves on to the next complaining customer. This is why too much of "customer service" these days is reactionary and process driven, with managers and service staff monitored and measured in terms of efficiencies, quickness of response, and the number of complaints "handled" per shift, day, week, or month.

When complaints are handled and tracked this way, true organizational learning and the opportunity to turn complaints into new levels of customer satisfaction through positive change are usually lost. Forever. Or at least until an enlightened new manager takes over the so-called customer service unit.

Lastly, it is important to remember that all complainers have one of two things in common — they are all *customers* or *prospects*.

Service recovery starts with the way you handle complaints and complainers, a topic that we discuss in the *Powerful Marketing Memos* on *Make it Easy for Customers to Complain* and *Types and Modes of Customer Complaints*.

Until then, remember that complaints are good. And that, for the most part, people who complain are customers who truly care about your future. Or at least your future with them as your customers.

Key Point: customers who complain are customers who care.

Taking Action: how are customer complaints handled in your organization? Are they processed and handled as quickly and efficiently as possible, and then forgotten? What steps are needed to turn the efficient handling of complaints into learning opportunities for your organization?

How is customer service monitored and measured in your organization? What does your customer service "scorecard" look like? Does it include measurements for how lessons from the frontline are circulated to other staff, used in training courses, and incorporated into new employee orientation programs?

How can lessons from the frontline be turned into *learning stories* to the benefit of the entire organization and its customers?

Make it Easy for Customers to Complain

Two of the key points from the prior *Powerful Marketing Memo* titled *Complaints Are Good* are: 1) complaints will happen because mistakes will happen, and 2) customers who complain are customers who care.

Therefore, knowing that you are going to get complaints and knowing that such complaints are good for you, it makes sense to have a complaint management strategy in place that not only focuses on resolving the various customer issues that crop up but that also systematically turns customer complaints into learning opportunities for the entire organization.

The first component of your complaint management strategy is that you should **make it easy for customers to complain**.

"What?" I can hear many of you saying. "Make it easier for customers to complain, so that we actually get *more* complaints?"

But that's exactly what your goal should be — to drive in more complaints. After all, if you do not hear about the problems your customers are having with your products, services, or staff then how are you going to go about fixing these?

Secondly, when a customer has a complaint, and they run into hurdles and barriers trying to voice their complaint to someone, all they do is get angrier and angrier. The result is a small problem develops into a multi-faceted larger one, simply because the customer cannot find a way to channel their concerns, anger, fears, worries, questions, or complaints to your organization in a timely and convenient manner.

This is particularly true when it comes to the information posted on your website. Few things seem to infuriate customers more these days than not being able to find the right contact details on an organization's website for lodging a complaint, or for speaking to someone other than a call center "service rep."

Thus, there are two key benefits from making it easy for customers to complain:

1) your customers do not get angrier and more upset from the additional frustrations of trying to contact your organization, and

2) you have more opportunities to fix initial, small problems before they evolve into larger and harder to resolve ones.

Part of your complaint management strategy needs to emphasize to all employees, especially the first tier and second tier staff who routinely have to deal with 90% of customer complaints, that *service recovery starts with how you react to complaints.*

Unfortunately, for too many organizations the initial reaction to a customer complaint is either defensive (trying to push the blame back onto the customer) or process driven (having a focus on a speedy resolution so that the frontline service staff can rapidly move onto the next customer complaint).

This approach often has unintended negative consequences, as customers end up feeling that they have been handled in a non-personalized fashion or have been quickly served so that another customer's situation can take priority. This is not to say that speed and prompt resolutions are not appreciated; however it is important to understand that the manner in which swift results are delivered can be perceived as dehumanizing and robotic.

A good example of this is when an organization's email auto responder system sends out the highly depersonalizing *"thank you for your enquiry, we will get back to you promptly"* message when an email of complaint is sent via the organization's website. Please note: an email (or letter) of complaint **is not an enquiry**. It is an attempt to get a humanized and customized resolution to a situation that *your customer* find unpalatable. It should not be responded to in the same manner as an email asking a general product or service question.

Additionally, in the most unfortunate situations, another unintended negative consequence of the focus on speed is that the customer actually walks away feeling unheard and that his or her true, underlining complaint was not surfaced, ignored, overlooked, or not fully understood. The result is that customers feel it is difficult to voice their complaints to the organization, and may end up deciding that it is far easier to take their business elsewhere than to continue dealing with an organization that fails to listen and comprehend.

It is for this reason that I advocate changing *customer service staff* into *customer satisfaction staff,* who are then measured on their abilities to deliver complete satisfaction to customers, rather than by quantitative indicators such as the number of calls handled, the number of customers served, and the "average time per service transaction. It is not a matter of semantics, but of a philosophical approach of being fully customer focused and pro-active in the area of customer satisfaction, rather than being reactive and process driven in determining customer service standards.

One interesting thing I have noticed is that *customers are more acute listeners and observers when they are angry* and that they *notice every little detail about how they are being treated and what steps the organization is taking* to settle a dispute. As a result, each and every thing done by someone representing the organization, including outsourced contract staff such as those in call centers, is noted and mentally recorded by upset customers. This is especially true for any attempts to forestall the customer from complaining or to thwart their desires to be fully heard and understood.

Customers willingly play these details back to the next level of management, or to anyone else who will listen — including your other customers and prospects — at a moment's notice. This not only lengthens the time it takes to eventually solve the original customer complaint, but it also means the dissatisfactions incurred by the customer while engaged in the settlement process must now also be dealt with. This leads to additional costs to the organization, in terms of both staff hours and the eventual compensation to the customer, as well as an unsatisfying feeling all around for the customer, staff, and management.

All this could be alleviated, of course, if you simply made it easier for customers to complain in the first place.

In the next *Powerful Marketing Memo* we will share our thoughts on how to effectively handle informal and formal complaints.

In the meantime, whenever you receive a customer complaint be sure to *thank the customer for their feedback* and use this situation as an opportunity to re-dedicate your staff to eliminating the problems, errors, mistakes, and other factors that cause customer complaints rather than trying to just eliminate the complaints themselves.

Handling customer complaints properly impacts all current and future customers — and starts with processes, procedures, and systems that make it easy for such complaints to be communicated to your organization.

So, make it easy and convenient for your customers to complain. You will be glad you did. For the benefits will be for you and the organization to reap.

Key Point: make it easy for customers to complain to your organization.

Taking Action: how are customer complaints handled in your organization? Are they processed and handled as quickly and efficiently as possible, and then forgotten? What can be done so that customer complaints are fully voiced and understood?

What steps are needed to turn the efficient handling of complaints into learning opportunities for your organization?

How is customer service monitored and measured in your organization? What does your customer service "scorecard" look like? Does it include measurements for how lessons from the frontline are circulated to other staff, used in training courses, and incorporated into new employee orientation programs?

Types and Modes of Customer Complaints

As we all know, customer complaints will happen. While elimination of customer complaints may be a desired state, in truth this is nothing other than an illusionary goal.

And besides, the true goal should be the elimination of errors, mistakes, and other factors that cause customer dissatisfaction. If you eliminate customer complaints, without eradicating the errors producing the displeasure and discontent for your customers, you will effectively wipe out a very important channel of customer feedback that can be critical in helping your organization make needed improvements.

Since customer complaints are a given, I find it useful to break these down and to categorize the types of complaints that are most often received. For me, the following six categories work best for identifying and classifying types of customer complaints:

Informative — when the customer informs you that a mistake has been made. This is usually done to help you prevent making the same mistake again. In this case, the customer is dissatisfied, but not enough to request that remedial action be taken or an offer of compensation made. Often it is about a "little thing" and typically is about something that is too late to change or fix (or something that the customer has already fixed). For instance, a comment made when paying the bill at a restaurant such as *the vegetables were a bit undercooked today* or a statement made when checking out of a hotel such as *housekeeping didn't put any hand towels in my room last night.*

Corrective — when the customer informs you about a mistake and expects corrective action to be taken (often immediately). This type of complaint is made as the customer is dissatisfied and wants to have this dissatisfaction eliminated through some action. As a rule the customer is looking for the mistake to be fixed and the situation remedied, rather than for some level of compensation. In other words, when a customer calls housekeeping or the hotel operator to complain about missing hand towels, they are looking for someone to promptly deliver the hand towels to the room. In such a situation they do not expect to be upgraded to a suite or have a discount applied to the room charge. Promptness of resolution, in these situations, is key.

Experiential — when the customer relates to you their personal experience or experiences with your products or services. This type of complaint is often hard to judge, particularly in the early stages of the conversation. The customer may simply be explaining their situation and trying to find out if this is a normal occurrence. On the other hand, they may be communicating what happened as an indication that their expectations were not met. Sometimes they may even just be "blowing off a bit of steam" and, once having gotten the situation off their chest, may be ready to move on to more important things. However, sometimes they are not ready to move on and want you to focus on what has happened to them. The best thing to do in this situation is to actively listen and then re-classify the experience into one of the other five types of customer complaints.

Unsatisfied — here the customer complaint is focused on their perception that your products or services did not meet their expectations. And thus they are unsatisfied with their purchase or with your service performance. In this case, both corrective action and compensation are probably demanded. Interestingly, the compensation is sought in "payment" for the customer's time in seeking a resolution and for *taking the time to explain the problem to you and your staff.* I highlight this last phrase for it supports what we wrote in *Complaints Are Good* —customers who complain are customers who care. But by caring, and by taking the time to care and complain, they expect some sort of compensation, which can take the form of a discount, a free gift, the provision of some extra level of service, or even a coupon for a discount on a future purchase.

Societal — here the customer has found the actions of one of your staff members to be unbecoming or unacceptable. What the customer is usually seeking are two things: a) an apology and b) punishment or reprimanding of the staff. As this type of complaint is another form of dissatisfaction, both corrective action and some level of compensation are normally sought.

Conflict — this occurs when the customer has "had it up to HERE" and has now become your organizational or personal enemy, either overtly, subvertly, or covertly. Obviously, you have a major problem on your hands and in such situations it is best to escalate this matter up your management hierarchy as quickly as possible for a resolution (however unlikely) or for containment.

By categorizing any customer complaint into one of the six categories above, you will be in a better position to craft an effective solution and remedy that not only resolves the issue from your customer's perspective but one that also helps you build stronger bonds with that customer.

There are two modes of complaints, and understanding the differences between the two will also help your staff handle customer complaints more effectively. These modes, and the characteristics of each, are:

Informal — almost always delivered to the frontline service person or one level above and delivered orally in an informal manner such as a chat or a short phone call to a manager, supervisor, or the call center. If sent by writing, this mode of customer complaint will be found on a customer comment card, a service delivery questionnaire, or a short email.

Formal — if delivered orally in a face-to-face situation it will usually be done one to two management levels above the frontline service person, in a serious tone dictated by the customer. If delivered in writing, it will typically be sent as a letter to a customer service supervisor, store manager, or other middle management level. If delivered orally via the telephone, the customer will likely request to speak with the call center supervisor or to a customer service manager.

One of my personal marketing cornerstones is that *preventing customer complaints is better than resolving them.* Such prevention, however, must come through quality products, services, procedures, processes, policies, and staff. This does not imply that you should prevent customer complaints from being *fully voiced and understood.*

When something goes wrong, it is best to hear about it. Only the problems your organization hears and knows about are fixable.

A lack of customer complaints is not necessarily a sign that your organization is performing extremely well. It might actually be an indication that your customers no longer care enough about you to complain, or do not feel it is worthwhile any more to complain, and instead are taking their business elsewhere.

The mantra for this week, and every week, is simply *customer complaints are good!*

Key Point: whether delivered informally or formally, most customer complaints can be categorized as informative, corrective, experiential, unsatisfied, societal, or conflict.

Taking Action: whenever you receive a customer complaint be sure to *thank the customer for their feedback* and use this situation as an opportunity to re-dedicate your staff to eliminating the problems, errors, mistakes, and other factors that cause customer complaints rather than trying to just eliminate the complaints themselves.

Start a log of all customer complaints received in the next month. What percent are delivered formally? Informally? How do the informal complaints differ from the formal ones?

Categorize these complaints into the six types of complaints outlined above. How does your method of handling each type of complaint differ? Why? Where can improvements be made?

Analyze your method of handling complaints. When is compensation offered to customers? Is there a noticeable pattern? Is this done consistently and routinely? Why or why not?

Supporting Your Customer Service Reps

As customers feel it is their right to have 24x7 customer service availability for more and more product categories and industries, the role of the customer service representative takes on even greater importance.

I wonder, though, based on my experience of dealing with customer service reps, how many companies ever sit down and explain in detail product specifications, the rules and regulations of contests and promotions, or even details of the latest promotion or product advertising? Not many, it seems.

This neglect of the customer service staff is absolutely mind-boggling.

Despite all the books, articles, seminars, workshops, and customer service gurus advocating the importance of customer service, customer care, and even customer intimacy, it appears that very little thought, training, or motivation goes toward the frontline customer service staff in many organizations.

Your customer service reps should be given the same details and briefing as your sales staff. After all, the customer service staff are often in more frequent contact with your customers than the sales staff, and hence they have more opportunities to cross-sell or up-sell to your customers. As mentioned in the *Powerful Marketing Memo* on the Sales/Service Relationship, *every service opportunity is a sales opportunity.*

And, as I like to continually point out, customer service representatives should, in fact, be trained and motivated as customer *satisfaction* representatives.

Many managers don't like to invest training funds in customer service representatives, as they say there's always too high a turnover rate in this area. Of course, this begs the question, "might not a decent training program and an exciting incentive program **decrease turnover** within the customer service area?"

It's also important to remember that customer service reps can provide a valuable two-way service — by communicating to customers all the possible solutions the company offers, and by communicating back to management all the good and bad news they hear from customers. But the latter takes place only when you have an inherent feedback and debriefing process in place. This sort of customer feedback rarely makes it back to senior management if the debriefing process is not formal and conducted regularly (like weekly).

Likewise, the debriefing sessions for customer service reps should also focus on two-way communication. From management's perspective, these sessions (which I recommend as small group sessions) should be used to encourage continuous feedback, to provide answers and information to help the reps perform their jobs better, and to recognize how important the reps (and their work) are to the company.

From the rep's perspective, the debriefing sessions should give them sufficient time to report back on the customer comments they are hearing, and for the group to discuss whether the comments concern isolated events or if any trends are developing. The sessions should be open and honest forums, where the reps feel free to bring up any issues and to report back on any concerns being raised by customers.

While the immediate supervisor of the customer service reps is best placed to hold these regular debriefing sessions, it is always good for more senior management to attend occasionally. This reinforces the importance of the sessions and also gives senior management an opportunity to hear unfiltered reports from their frontline troops.

Nothing in this process should convey the message that the customer service area is a glorified complaint department. You want to encourage both positive and negative feedback, and to treat the customer service team as your market and customer reconnaissance team.

Remember, the customer service representative is often the first, and the last, person representing the company that the customer talks to. Shouldn't these be some of the most motivated, trained, and enthusiastic people on your staff?

Key Point: treat your customer service representatives like a first-rate team and you will receive first-rate customer and market intelligence.

Taking Action: how good a job are you doing of keeping your customer service representatives informed and up-to-date on products, promotions, customer issues? How could this be improved?

What is your turnover rate for CSRs? If it is too high, you might consider using an outside resource to conduct interviews with some who left to identify true causes of the turnover rate.

How do customers rate your CSRs? What needs improvement? Why?

Taking Care of Customers

I was in Melbourne one year attending a major meeting of the Australian and New Zealand banks that issue MasterCard credit cards and Maestro debit cards.

Mr. Nicholas Utton, Chief Marketing Officer of MasterCard International at the time, had one key message for this audience of senior bankers concerning customers: "If we don't take care of our customers, someone else will."

That's worth repeating....and reflecting on: "If we don't take care of our customers, someone else will."

And how true that is. Just think about all the choices and options available to customers today. Rare is the organization that finds itself without competitors. Even rarer is the customer that finds himself without options, choices, or substitute products for the solutions they seek.

To take care of your customers, you need to have a full understanding of their wants, needs, and desires. I would also suggest that you need to have a corporate attitude that understands a person or an organization is not truly your customer until *the second time they buy.*

That's right. I recommend you do not consider anyone a customer until the second time they buy from you. The first time they buy they are merely a trial user. Unless they achieve complete satisfaction from the purchase *and* the use of your product or service, they may be unlikely to repeat their business with you. Hence, taking care of the customer goes beyond the mere sales cycle and includes all post-purchase activities such as use, repair, servicing, customer service, warranties, and trade-in or re-sale.

The best way to take care of your prospects and customers is to tailor or customize your products and service offering as much as you profitably can. Treat your customers as individuals....with individual needs, wants, desires, likes, and dislikes....at all customer touch points and you will be well on your way to developing customer loyalty.

And remember, in the words of MasterCard's former Chief Marketing Officer, if you don't take care of your customers, someone else will.

Key Point: if you don't take care of your customers, someone else will.

Taking Action: are you fully aware of the experiences customers have with your products? How satisfying are these experiences? Any way to find out?

Where can your product or service offers be customized? How can you create tailored solutions for your very, very important customers?

How can you find out if a first-time customer is likely to buy from you again? What kinds of communications can you put in place to evolve first-time buyers into repeat customers?

Importance of Customer Retention

Many organizations place their highest emphasis on attracting and gaining new customers.

While this is important, I feel it is more important to place an even higher emphasis on retaining and keeping your current customers. This is particularly true in saturated markets and industries, where your customers have many, many alternatives available to them.

Numerous research studies have shown that if you can reduce your attrition rate....that is the annualized rate of lost customers....by as little as five percentage points, you can increase your bottom-line profits by anywhere from 25% to 85%.

That's right, just keeping more of the customers you have, and preventing them from taking their business elsewhere, can have an immediate, positive impact on your bottom line profits.

The two best ways to keep customers from leaving are:

1) understanding their needs, and

2) delivering upon the promises you make to satisfy these needs.

What is the worst thing that happens when a customer leaves? It is not just that you lose the revenue, and profits, from that customer this year. It is also that you are likely to lose all future income from that customer, at least for several years to come. Lost customers rarely return. And certainly not quickly.

But the worst thing may not be just the lost revenue impact on your sales figures. The worst thing is that a typical customer will tell up to 19 people when they are dissatisfied with your products or services. Thus, your ability to transact, or to develop relationships, with these 19 other prospects and customers can be quickly diminished.

Another thing to remember is that not all customers are of equal value. Typically, a customer who has been with you for a longer time is more valuable than a more recently acquired customer. Research shows, for instance, that a customer who has been with you for five years is likely to be giving you 8-10 times the profit stream of a newly acquired customer.

Hence, if you lose a customer that has been buying from you for five years, you may need to replace that customer with not one, but perhaps 8-10 new customers just to replace the *value* of this one lost customer.

If there is one message you want to give your staff today, it may be a renewed emphasis on keeping and satisfying the customers you have.

Keeping good customers is a more sure-fire method for future success than a constant focus on attracting new customers.

Key Point: lost customers rarely return, and certainly not quickly. Thus the lost revenue stream from a lost customer is usually for several years, or forever.

Taking Action: what is your customer attrition level? How has this changed in the past 2-3 years? If you do not know, who should be assigned to study this issue?

What savings could you enjoy if you reduced your customer attrition levels and reduced your need for finding new customers?

Relationship Marketing

Relationship marketing is a concept that has yet to be clearly defined by anyone, even though much of today's marketing literature and many marketing consultants and gurus are in agreement that relationship marketing will be a critical success factor for the large majority of organizations.

I won't attempt to define relationship marketing here, but I will give you what I consider are the key elements of any strong relationship marketing program. These are:

- Understanding customer needs.
- Relevant product offer at appropriate time.
- Relevant reward at appropriate time.
- Relevant surprise at appropriate time.
- Two-way, interactive communication.
- Forward looking, long-term, bi-mutual engagement.

Whenever I think of the third and fourth points — giving a relevant reward or a relevant surprise at an appropriate time, I remember what happened to a close friend of mine.

This friend is a very heavy traveler and has a MasterCard credit card from one of the banks here in Singapore. This bank decided to give him an end of the year present, and sent him a lovely hamper gift containing two bottles of wine and a box of chocolates.

Nice, right? The only problem is that neither my friend, nor his wife, drinks wine. And neither are big chocolate eaters either!

This bank thinks it has a good relationship with my friend because he is a heavy spender on their MasterCard card. But they don't know enough about him *as an individual* to truly have a relationship with him.

How much easier — and smarter — it would have been for the bank to call my friend on the phone and say: "We would like to say thank you for your large volume of business with us on your MasterCard credit card. Your business is very important to us and we would like to say thank you by presenting you with either two bottles of wine and a box of chocolates, or a gift certificate so that you can take your wife out to dinner. *Which would you prefer?"*

Your gifts of appreciation need to be relevant to your customer.

And since not all customers have the same likes and preferences, you need to check in advance before you send them a gift. Otherwise, your efforts in relationship building will backfire on you.

By the way, I do enjoy both wine and chocolate, so if I am your customer, feel free to send these my way any time!

Key Point: your gifts of appreciation need to be relevant to your customer.

Taking Action: do you reward all your customers, or all your "VIP" customers, the same way? Do you send everyone the same seasonal gift? Why?

How do you track differences in preferences, likes, and dislikes among your most important customers?

What effort would it take for your organization to identify the top 15% most important customers and then to start identifying ways to *individually* approach, understand, and reward these customers?

Truly Understanding Customer Needs

I write and speak often of the need for frontline staff (and actually *all* staff as well) to *fully understand and appreciate* customer needs. And, simultaneously, I encourage management to develop *flexible* policies and procedures so that their staff can handle customer needs and concerns *on an individual basis*.

Here's a true story that brings all these points succinctly together.

A man in Singapore applied for a Platinum MasterCard card from one of the issuing banks. His documentation proved that he earned above the S$150,000 per year, which the bank had set as the minimum income level for this premium product.

Upon receiving approval for his Platinum MasterCard, he requested a Platinum supplementary card for his wife and a Gold supplementary card for his 18-year old daughter who was about to depart for college in Melbourne, Australia.

The frontline customer service officer had no problem in approving the supplementary card for his wife, but told this customer that she could not issue a Gold supplementary card for his daughter as "It's *our policy* that only Platinum supplementary cards can be issued for Platinum accounts."

If one understands how the computer systems are established that support card center businesses, one can understand why this policy is in place. It has to do with the way account numbers and product codes are entered and stored in the system. Hence, I have no issue with the policy, per se.

The key issues, to my marketing eyes and ears, are two-fold:

- the frontline person obviously took little effort to *fully understand* **why** the customer was making this particular request, and hence could not *appreciate* this customer's **particular needs and concerns**, and

- the bank did not allow any *flexibility* in its policies and procedures, and hence the frontline person was left **with little maneuverability** in trying to satisfy the needs of this customer.

Now, if you are a parent, you can probably instinctively understand and empathize with a person who does not want to send his 18-year off to college with a *Platinum* credit card. This has nothing to do with the credit limit assigned to this card, for that can be controlled by the customer and the bank. But it does *have a lot* to do with how his daughter may be perceived by her peers and friends at a university in a foreign country (i.e. as a spoiled little rich kid?).

Unfortunately, the frontline staff handling this customer was not a parent and thus could not honestly fathom **why** the customer was insisting on an exception to the bank's policy. (Note: it is often best to have your frontline staff mirror your customer base in terms of demographic composition, thus improving the odds that they will understand one another better.)

As a result, the customer declined to accept the Platinum MasterCard card from this bank and went elsewhere in search of a satisfactory solution to his needs.

Even worse, as I later discovered, this particular bank did have a policy of **waiving** the annual Gold card fees for its Platinum cardholders. In other words, the frontline customer service staff could have issued **a free** Gold MasterCard card to this customer, in addition to issuing his Platinum card. Then, the wife's supplementary card could have been linked to the Platinum account and the daughter's supplementary card linked to the Gold account. And the customer would have had two products to use, or not use, as he chose.

Unfortunately, there was no "out of the box" thinking and a potentially very loyal and profitable customer was lost.

Can you read this story and honestly say to yourself, "there but for the grace of good fortune goes our organization?" Or is there a likelihood that your customers and prospective customers may be facing similar situations of not being fully understood, and not having their needs fully appreciated?

Key Point: customer needs and concerns need to be **fully** understood and appreciated by all staff.

Taking Action: how flexible are your policies? Are you losing customers due to inflexibility?

Two of the most important skills for frontline staff are listening and empathy. How does your staff rate on these two skills? Is it time for a refresher course?

Put a mirror in front of any comments "our customers do not understand us" and see if the opposite is also true — that your staff do not understand your customers.

Survey your customers and ask them if they feel your staff truly understand their needs.

Customer Retention: The Art of Keeping Good Customers™

The world in which marketing takes place has changed, and continues to change at a rapid pace.

Customers, customer needs, and the individual motivations for making purchasing decisions are also changing. The natural loyalty of customers is a thing of the past, not just because customers have become more fickle but also because the large majority of organizations do not exhibit any tendencies that deserve customer loyalty.

As customers become more knowledgeable about the options available to them, as well as more aware and understanding about their own individual wants, needs, and desires, the more they want to be recognized and understood as individuals. Without a doubt, customers give their business — and more important their *repeat business* — to the organizations that do the best job of understanding and responding to their *individual* wants, needs, and desires.

In this highly competitive marketing environment, organizations need to move from a transaction-focus and product-line focus to a *customer focus*. Highly successful firms take this a step further, by developing techniques to continuously learn from interactions with customers. They also implement procedures that enable them to deepen customer relationships by properly responding to the insights gained from these interactions.

Early attempts at this direction have often gone wrong, for the simple reason that the global CRM movement convinced many senior executives that customer relationships could be *managed*.

No customer I have ever spoken with wants to have their relationship with a selling organization *managed*. The whole concept of taking an economic view of customers that measures the profitability of each individual customer and then attempting to manage (i.e. grow) those relationships that the organization finds to be profitable is, at best, one-sided and valid for short durations only.

In these highly expensive, technology-led CRM implementations, customer relationships are defined by product ownership levels, size of orders, and cross-selling opportunities. While all valid parameters from an organization's perspectives, none of these are the key ways in which customers would primarily define *their relationships* with the organizations with which they do business.

Not surprisingly, customers actually want their relationships to be nurtured, cultivated, appreciated, cherished, and looked after. Anything but managed!

One of my personal goals is to help organizational leaders move beyond the primeval and self-centered goals currently being practiced in many operations to a business philosophy that is more likely to help retain the customer relationships critical to continued success. At the heart of this philosophy, which I call *the art of keeping good customers,* is the changing of the acronym CRM to mean Customer Retention Marketing.

Customer retention has a direct impact on corporate profitability. As one often-cited report in the *Harvard Business Review* showed, a decrease of just five percentage points in customer attrition can increase bottom-line profitability by 25% to 80% across a wide range of industries.

This makes your own customer base is a highly under-valued asset.

How important is the issue of customer retention? Another *Harvard Business Review* article stated that "the average U.S. corporation loses one-half of their customers every five years and these (attrition) rates stunt corporate growth by up to 35 percent."

It is little wonder that an Economist Intelligent Unit article *Managing Customer Relationships* reported that "the number of businesses citing 'customer retention' as a critically important measure in the next five years has jumped to nearly 60%, as companies shift their focus from attracting new customers to retaining their more profitable ones."

Successful companies today are switching from a transaction perspective with their customers to a customer loyalty-building perspective. The way to do this is to earn customer loyalty, by understanding true customer needs, committing to quality, delivering upon the promises you make, and by treating customers as people, not as accounts.

In the past, being customer-oriented has meant operating in order to meet the needs of the *typical* customer, or the average customer.

Fewer and fewer businesses today can afford to focus on the average customer. Your future growth, and future profitability, comes from fully satisfying the needs of your most valuable customers.

To treat your most valuable customers *not as average customers*, but as *your most valued customers*, requires that they be treated as individuals — with individual needs, wants, desires, likes, and dislikes.

This is the true essence behind the concept of *the art of keeping good customers.* ™

Key Point: you need to treat your most valuable customers not as average customers but as your most valued customers.

Taking Action: what is the focus of your marketing efforts, to win new customers or to keep your good customers? Why?

What benefits could be gained from moving a portion of your marketing budget to reduce customer attrition? Would these benefits be significantly increased if you reallocated a significant portion of the marketing budget to customer retention?

Do you measure the costs of lost customers? If not, how could you?

Which do your employees think is more important: keeping current customers or finding new customers? Why? Is this the best emphasis given your current and anticipated market conditions?

The 7 Laws of True CRM

I have long struggled with the concept of Customer Relationship Management (CRM), mostly for the simple reason that I fully understand that customers *do not* want their relationships with an organization "managed."

This is why the whole notion and philosophy of CRM as customer relationship management is wrong.

One of my key messages has long been that marketers and senior management need to think of CRM as **Customer Retention Marketing**.

This is what *true* CRM is all about – retaining customers, or as I like to call it: *the art of keeping good customers.*™

To implement this better definition of CRM in your organization, you need to inculcate the following 7 Laws of True CRM into your culture, processes, and thinking:

1. The conversion of a prospect to a purchaser *is the casting of a potential long-term relationship with a possible customer.* A purchaser who buys from

you the first time is merely a trial user. A customer is not **a true customer** until the second time they buy from you. Forget the notions that "the relationship starts with a purchase," or "you are not closing a sale, you are starting a relationship." As we pointed out many times, the relationship starts way back in the information seeking stage of the buying cycle, at least from the customer's perspective.

The art of keeping good customers means that your entire organization should be geared to ensure that every experience received by a customer (including a first-time purchaser) should result in that customer repeating their future purchases from you whenever you have a product or solution that meets their needs or solves a problem for them.

2. You do not work for your employer — you work for your customers. Sure, someone in the company signs your proverbial paycheck (or most likely authorizes the

direct deposit into your bank account). But those checks and deposits would bounce if it weren't for the customers who buy from your organization. When someone asks you "who do you work for?" your reply should be "our customers" or "the customers of (name of organization).

3. You do not sell products or services — you sell solutions that meet the needs, wants, and desires of your customers. As pithy as this sounds, it is something that way too many organizations and workers these days just do not seem to understand.

4. Customers want relationships with people and organizations they trust, that are committed to them, and with whom they have shared goals. All of us can buy products and services from a vast number of suppliers and outlets. But we choose to have continual relationships, and to repeat our business, with those we

trust and with those whom we have shared outcomes.

5. Employees should be liberated — and allowed to be customer champions. Almost all staff want to serve customers well, if only their organizations would let them! Unfortunately too many organizations have rules, processes, procedures, and policies that tie the hands of their employees and prevent them from truly serving customers and satisfying their wants, needs, and desires.

6. Do not have a commitment to customer service — **have a commitment to customers.** Customers have too many choices and options available to them. But they also all share a deficit of sufficient time. Caring about customers means committing to the things customers place high value on — flexibility, sufficient knowledge and information, convenience, ability to choose functions relevant to them,

customization, and environmental concerns.

And, of course, good service, which in today's world is now a prerequisite for repeat business as customers will simply not put up with bad service, inconvenience, inflexible policies and procedures, or a lack of easily available options for customization and personalization.

7. Customer Service staff should be fired — and replaced with Customer Satisfaction staff. This is not a matter of semantics. Customer service tends to be either reactive (to a situation) or a follow-up activity (to a complaint). Customer service, which is problem resolution focused, is usually initiated by the customer, when he or she has a problem. On the other hand, customer satisfaction is proactive and is customer focused. Customer satisfaction is usually initiated by the organization to improve the quality of the relationship with the

customer. The corollary of this rule is that customer service scorecards, measurements, and matrixes should be replaced with indices that measure and monitor customer satisfaction.

In the typical CRM thinking found today, the organization is the center of focus, thinking, and planning. And the measurement tools used are indicators that support managerial bonuses.

In my Customer Retention Marketing model, the customer is the focus and occupies the central platform for all thinking, planning, and strategic focus. The result becomes the optimization of customer-first processes and the continued improvement in the quality of customer interactions.

Your organization will accomplish a great deal more, and will be more highly successful, by changing your definition of CRM to **Customer Retention Marketing**.

Key Point: change your definition of CRM to mean Customer Retention Marketing.

Taking Action: survey your employees and ask them this open-ended question: "what do we sell to customers?" If they give you a long list of products and services it is time to educate them that you are selling solutions and benefits, not products and services.

Review the tools and measurements you use to track and monitor customer service. How could these be turned into tools and measurements to track and monitor customer satisfaction?

Prepare an entire issue of your next employee newsletter (or staff memo) on the subject of customer retention marketing, and what the implications are for the organization in terms of customer care, customer satisfaction measurements, liberating of customer contact personnel, changes in policies and procedures, and how you will reward the organization for making the change to customer retention marketing.

Survey the top 20% of your customers on their perceptions of how well your organization delivers customer satisfaction. Survey 100% of your employees asking the same questions. Compare the results.

Building Customer Loyalty

How do you build customer loyalty?

To start with, your organization has to be able to fully understand customer requirements and to appreciate customer needs....particularly individual customer needs.

And you need to have policy flexibility and organizational adaptability in order to meet individual customer needs. In other words, you need to be flexible in how your policies are applied. Not all customers are equal or alike....and therefore you cannot afford to treat all customers equally or in the same manner.

To fully understand customer requirements and needs, you need to engage in interactive, two-way, on-going dialogues with your customers. Now, of course, you probably cannot afford to do this with each and every one of your customers. Particularly if you have a large customer base.

But your organization should be engaging in two-way, interactive dialogues with your most important customers. And you should have a dedication to complete quality control throughout your organization.

The best way to build customer loyalty is by completely satisfying the needs of your critical customers. A commitment to quality control is essential if you are to completely satisfy your customers.

Why do your repeat customers continue to transact with you? Is this because you are the most convenient option? Because you are the lowest price? Or because you completely satisfy their needs?

If the answer is anything except the latter, then your business is vulnerable to an astute competitor — who can beat you by focusing on this one criterion. However, if you are providing true customer satisfaction, then I would not even attempt to compete with you!

Remember, customer satisfaction is both more anticipatory and pro-active than is mere customer service.

First, it seeks to understand what your customer's needs are and then to ensure that they are fully satisfied, not merely mollified with a quick-fix solution or an apologetic reward or gift aimed to pacify an unhappy customer.

Second, customer satisfaction is a mindset that seeks to anticipate future customer needs and therefore prevents the organization from making future mistakes and errors.

Best of all....if you are anticipating future customer needs you are undoubtedly doing the one most important thing that will build customer loyalty....taking care of the customer's needs before he or she even recognizes those needs. That's how you truly build customer loyalty.

Key Point: customer satisfaction is both more anticipatory and pro-active than is mere customer service.

Taking Action: what are your customer service goals and standards? Are these reactive and customer service focused (i.e. time spent serving each customer, average customer wait time, etc.) or are they designed so that you deliver CUSTOMER SATISFACTION at each point of customer contact?

What can you do to make CUSTOMER SATISFACTION your key point of differentiation?

Earning Customer Loyalty

How do you earn customer loyalty?

Think about how you, as an individual, are loyal to any of the establishments or businesses where you are willing to repeat purchase. What does it take to make *you* a loyal customer?

It is probably the same thing that it takes to make any of us....including your own customers....loyal.

And that is a commitment to quality and a dedication to delivering upon the promises made by the organization.

I believe that it is a very straightforward equation that starts with quality and results in customer loyalty. Simply put, this equation is:

Quality will result in customer satisfaction.

Customer satisfaction....true customer satisfaction....will result in repeat purchases.

And repeat purchases will lead directly to customer loyalty.

Remember, we are talking about customer satisfaction here, not customer mollification, customer happiness, or even customer delight.

Someone asked me recently, "What is the difference between customer delight and customer satisfaction."

That is a good question. I believe that customer delight is a short-term experience, one that is usually experienced as a result of some extra niceness or courtesy performed by a seller's staff. It is something that surpasses the customer's expectations at the time it is received or experienced.

While there's nothing wrong with customer delight....it does not have the same long lasting effect as customer satisfaction.

Customer satisfaction, on the other hand, comes from the buying experience, the usage experience, and the post-purchase experience received by the customer while buying, using, or consuming your product.

If you want your customers to be repeat customers....and therefore loyal customers....focus on making them completely satisfied.

A little customer delight never hurts....but do not make that the end-all and be-all of your customer satisfaction efforts.

After all, the key difference between a trial user and a loyal customer is that the loyal customer keeps coming back to repeat his or her business with you.

Key Point: if you want your customers to be repeat customers — and therefore loyal customers — focus on making them completely satisfied.

Taking Action: are your quality standards designed to truly achieve Complete Customer Satisfaction? When was the last time you researched the needs of your customers to see if they are Completely Satisfied?

What percent of your customer base is loyal? What percent of your annual revenue comes from repeat customers? If you don't know the answer to these two questions, I highly recommend you assign someone to go find out.

What can you do to make COMPLETE CUSTOMER SATISFACTION your key point of competitive differentiation and customer loyalty enhancement?

Rewarding Customer Loyalty

It is important to reward customer loyalty....but we have to be careful not to bribe customers into loyalty.

It is kind of like raising children. Once you start to "bribe" your child, as in "if you eat everything on your plate tonight you will get a cookie," there is no ending to the bribe. This one cookie for a clean plate trick works for a week or two, and then the bribe has to be increased to two cookies, or even three, before the child will willingly complete his or her entire meal.

Many marketers are making the same mistake when it comes to developing so-called loyalty programs. The airlines were one of the first to make this error. Once one airline started to capture greater market share with a frequent flier program, everyone else added similar programs. Now, practically all airlines offer some kind of a mileage "loyalty" program.

There is little differentiation between these programs, and hence many passengers (and certainly most frequent fliers) are no more loyal to one airline than they were previously. Frequent fliers tend to belong to multiple FFP programs. And now with 2-3 major alliances being formed in the industry, it is easy for everyone to belong to these 2-3 Super League FFPs. So where's the point of differentiation? There isn't one!

All that has happened is that the cost of business has been raised for all players in the airline industry.

We have seen the same thing happen here in Singapore in the petrol and credit card markets. It seems like all the petrol stations, and certainly all the banks offering credit cards, have developed some sort of rewards scheme under the guise of loyalty marketing. It is no wonder that Singaporeans tend to carry credit cards from 3-4 banks in their wallets and purses, and that they switch from one petrol rewards scheme to another — depending upon the prizes offered — on a regular basis.

These are not rewards programs. They are customer bribery programs and all they do is raise the cost of business for everyone in these particular industries.

And, like the getting the child to eat their dinner....the cost of such programs goes in only one direction — up!

Smart marketers will develop loyalty programs that truly reward customers....not attempt to bribe them.

Key Point: it is important to reward customer loyalty, but be careful not to turn your customer loyalty programs into customer bribery programs.

Taking Action: how do you reward customer loyalty? Is it with products and services that fully satisfy customer needs, or with points programs that attempt to bribe customers into loyalty?

How easy is it for your competitors to match your loyalty scheme?

Do your customers switch back and forth between you and competitors based on the promotional programs being offered? If so, how can you start to compete based on true customer satisfaction, rather than to continue to engage in tactical marketing wars?

If you were a customer of your company, what would entice you to be the most loyal customer in the world? Can this enticement be applied to your customers today?

Keeping Customers Loyal

Keeping customers loyal is an art form, not a science.

As is true of all good marketing practices. Marketing is, after all, an art, not a scientific discipline.

The most important ways to keep customers loyal are five simple....simple to understand I should say....but not always simple to execute....actions:

1. Always deliver upon the promises that anyone in the organization makes. Walk your talk. Have everyone in the organization understand that your word is your bond with customers.

2. Ensure that you have consistent product and service delivery at all times.

3. Anticipate future customer needs — and create flexible, adaptable and customer-focused organizational structures so that you are better prepared to meet these changing customer needs *before* they occur.

4. Solve future customer needs — either through changing product features, benefits, or through upgraded service delivery.

5. Cultivate long-term, bi-mutual customer relationships by being engaged in two-way, interactive dialogues with your customers that help you anticipate their changing and future needs.

Naturally, you cannot....and probably do not want....to cultivate deep-seated relationships with all your customers. The cost of doing so is probably prohibitive.

On the other hand, you certainly will want to apply these practices to the 20% of your customers who give you 80% of your revenues....or, better yet, the 80% of your profits....if you are able to calculate profitability on a customer-by-customer basis.

Customer loyalty needs to be thought of as a two-way street. Many senior managers and business owners I speak with these days complain that "customers are not as loyal as they used to be."

Then, when I start to investigate their own policy changes, pricing methodologies, and marketing activities, it becomes very obvious to me that many of these same organizations are no longer as loyal *to their customers* as they used to be.

No wonder they feel they have lost customer loyalty. They have stopped earning and deserving it through their own practices.

By following the five practices mentioned above, you will be in a better position to ensure that you do not suffer from deteriorating customer loyalty.

Key Point: keeping customers loyal is an art, not a science. But there are five proven steps you can take to practice this art.

Taking Action: does your organization always, constantly, live up to its word? Do you always deliver upon your promises?

Is there any pattern to inconsistency in your product or service delivery?

How do you anticipate future customer needs? How are these communicated and internalized within the organization?

Keeping Good Customers: The Sales/Service Ratio

As we approach the next era of marketing excellence, one which I often describe in terms of Relationship Marketing, companies need to learn how to apply a Zero Attrition Strategy as the foundation for their customer-focused marketing programs.

Keeping good customers loyal to your products, your services, and your organization is critical to your future marketing success. Having a loyal customer base of *good customers* (i.e. profitable ones who appreciate your products and services) will be one of your most competitive advantages with customers in this new era of marketing excellence.

The place to start is understanding why customers leave and how you can take steps to improve your customer retention ratios. The most successful companies in today's markets are doing a better job of retaining good customers by finding imaginative ways of exceeding customer expectations through the Sales/Service Relationship Formula. As a result, their competitors are finding it increasingly difficult to steal these entrenched customers.

The Sales/Service Relationship starts with a mindset of understanding and appreciating customer needs. It is not good enough to guess at what the customer's needs are. Your frontline people need to probe into these needs so that they can uncover the unspoken and deep-seated concerns of each individual customer. This will enable your sales force to turn service opportunities into sales and to turn sales opportunities into value-added service delivery.

At the heart of the Sales/Service Relationship is a commitment to quality — at all times and in all instances. It is a commitment that ensures that every little error, such as typos in your customer communications, are discovered and corrected *before* any customer is exposed to them. This includes email and websites. Ever notice how many emails you receive and websites you visit are loaded with spelling errors, despite the fact that most software today includes a basic spell checker application? There is no excuse — other than plain sloppiness and laziness — for this to happen.

Keeping customers truly loyal to your products and services requires more than numerous price discounts, decreasing margins, and "rewards" programs. To build relationships that last, your company must first *build* customer loyalty and *earn* customer loyalty, *before* attempts are made to reward customer loyalty. Most important, customer loyalty needs to be rewarded in a relevant manner, which means that not all customers should be rewarded equally or in the same manner.

Interestingly, loyal customers actually tend to be higher profit customers, and are often willing to pay higher margins in exchange for confidence and consistency of product and service delivery. This is where the organization's reputation and corporate image becomes so vital. A strong corporate image plays a significant role in both customer retention and customer loyalty. The corporate image can be a strategic weapon for any company, large or small, multinational or local.

Keeping good customers is a matter of being customer-centric in your marketing approach, understanding and applying the Sales/Service Relationship Formula, building relationships that last, and constantly leveraging your corporate brand for relationship building.

It may seem difficult, but it is a whole lot more rewarding (and profitable) than fighting your marketing battles over price, discounts, and channel rebates.

Key Point: developing a loyal base of good customers is a solid way to build long-term, consistent profitability.

Taking Action: how well does your frontline staff *appreciate* customer needs? I mean *truly* appreciate the needs and concerns of your key customers?

When was the last time you conducted a mystery shopper exercise with your frontline staff? Rather than test their product knowledge or their selling skills, isn't it time you tested their empathy and understanding skills?

How service-oriented are your sales people? How well versed in selling skills are your service people? How can any gaps be corrected?

Making Customer Loyalty Real for Manufacturers

Deloitte Research conducted a global manufacturing study in 1999 that resulted in an excellent report titled *Making Customer Loyalty Real: Lessons from Leading Manufacturers.*

Not only does the report state that "customer loyalty is a critical driver of shareholder value around the world," it also concludes that "for manufacturers, low price, high quality, and on-time delivery are no longer enough to stay in the game of global competition." What is imperative for future success, the study shows, is "the ability to anticipate and quickly adapt to changing customer demands."

"Our extensive study of the global manufacturing sector demonstrates that manufacturers must gear their entire organizations — not just their production operations — to attract profitable customers and retain them for life," states Deloitte. "The new game is about shifting from a product-centric to a customer-centric focus."

How do customer-centric manufacturers keep their customers loyal and deliver outstanding financial results? Well, according to Deloitte, the steps include superior performance in pricing, quality, sales and marketing, and customer service. In other words, the very criteria on which customers base their purchase decisions.

But there was one other aspect of the Deloitte report I found most fascinating. This had to do with the way in which customer loyalty actually strengthens the manufacturers' abilities to deliver on these key criteria. According to their analysis, "customer-centric manufacturers use their tight customer relationships to continually learn how to optimize investments across the customer interface and delight customers in their next interaction. In this way, customer loyalty creates more customer loyalty in a self-reinforcing cycle."

This research study supports my belief that customers are willing to enter into mutually rewarding, long-term loyalty relationships. The feeling that there is "no such thing as customer loyalty today" is a myth believed by those organizations trying to buy market share and by those that no longer act or behave in ways that encourage customer loyalty.

Without a doubt, customer loyalty is currently on a downtrend and seems to be decreasing across most product categories and industries. However, this is happening *not* because customers do not want to be loyal, *it is because most organizations today are not customer-centric and therefore do not act consistently in ways that encourage customer loyalty.*

There is a great opportunity awaiting the organization that can gear their entire operations — not just the sales and marketing staff, not just the customer service staff, not just the product and brand managers, but *everyone* — to being customer centric in all actions and behaviors.

Those who are doing it right — organizations like GE, Singapore Airlines, Qantas Airways, Amazon, Land's End, Nordstrom's, Apple, USAA, Best Buy, Avis, International SOS, and many others — are proof that when implemented correctly this is indeed a very powerful marketing and business model strategy. And those who are doing it wrong (sorry, but my lawyers won't let me list any examples — but you know who they are!), have seen their leadership positions erode, their market shares crumble, and their profitability come from focusing on cost management rather than market growth.

As the research by Deloitte shows, "manufacturers that do not enjoy strong customer relationships and are not organizationally integrated will find it increasingly difficult to keep up with changing customer demands and more responsive competitors. They will fall farther and farther behind manufacturers that are most customer-centric and whose competitive advantages continually improve."

All I can add to that is: this is doubly true for service organizations!

Customers want to conduct business with, and be loyal to, organizations that are overtly customer centric. Will yours be one of them?

Key Point: customer loyalty is a critical driver of shareholder value around the world.

Taking Action: on a scale of 1-10, rate your organization on being customer centric. Now rate your top three competitors. How do you compare?

What do customer-centric organizations do differently that yours is not doing today? What is worth replicating within your own organization?

Do you know the lifetime value of your customers or customer segments?

Can your customers settle all issues, including ordering, with just one phone call or one website visit?

Do you provide options for customers to select which services and channels they prefer to use?

Do you measure and set goals for customer loyalty?

Corporate Image Management

The corporate image is a dynamic and profound affirmation of the nature, culture, and structure of an organization. This applies equally to corporations, businesses large and small, government entities, and non-profit organizations.

Looked at from a marketing perspective, corporate brand management needs to be an on-going, synergistic management tool, rather than a one-time "corporate image exercise" as currently practiced by most organizations and almost all corporate identity consultants.

The corporate brand provides a mechanism for the organization to:

- Differentiate itself from competition.

- Create recognized added-value to the products and services marketed or delivered by the organization.

- Attract and maintain customer relationships in order to prosper in an increasingly competitive and constantly changing global marketplace.

The corporate image also represents the highest level of brand personality and characteristics that can be created and communicated to customers and marketing partners.

In today's world of deteriorating product brand power, rising perceptions of parity products, reducing employee loyalty, and increasing competition, the corporate brand image has taken on renewed importance.

Previously, a company's visual identity system was sufficient to project and protect the image of the organization. Today, all aspects of the corporate image need to be managed, from the refinement of the mission statement to how well the troops on the frontline understand, communicate, and portray this mission.

Corporate image management matches the expectations and understanding of both customers and employees about what the organization stands for, where it is heading, and what its core strengths, traditions and principles are.

The underlining principle of this discipline is simply this: **if it touches the customer, it's a marketing issue.™**

Nothing touches the customer more than how he or she **perceives** your corporate image. This fundamental perception will be the major factor that determines whether the customer will decide to conduct business with you and, more important, enter into a long-term and mutually rewarding relationship with your organization.

There may be no greater marketing issue than corporate image management in today's increasingly competitive markets. In short, corporate image management will be a key marketing discipline for years to come.

The ultimate battleground for winning and maintaining customer relationships now takes place in the minds, hearts, emotions, and *perceptions* of customers.

Key Point: the corporate image represents the highest level of brand personality and characteristics that can be created and communicated to customers and marketing partners.

Taking Action: where and how can you place greater resources in winning the battle for the minds, hearts, emotions, and perceptions of customers?

Is your corporate brand giving you sufficient differentiation in the market? Why or why not?

How can your corporate brand provide added value to the products and services marketed and delivered by the organization?

Corporate Image as a Powerful Tool

Every organization has a corporate image, whether it wants one or not.

When properly conceptualized, designed, and managed, the corporate image (and the resultant corporate brand) will accurately reflect the organization's commitment to quality, excellence, and its relationships with its various constituents: such as current and potential customers, employees and future staff, competitors, partners, governing bodies, and the general public.

As a result, the corporate image is a critical concern for every organization....one deserving the same attention and commitment by senior management as any other vital issue. Management of the corporate image and the corporate brand has become a core competency of the leaders and owners of the most successful organizations.

We live in a world of change. In fact, the rate of change today is faster, and affects a larger portion of the earth's population, than at any other time in history.

Yet, despite all this change, there is still one constant. And this is that marketing excellence and a strong corporate image are firmly linked. You cannot have one without the other. At least not for very long.

Because, at the end of the day....your competitors can mimic and better your product offer. They can create stronger distribution systems than yours. They can outspend you in advertising and promotions. And, of course, they can always beat you up on price.

But the one thing a competitor cannot mimic or copy is a well-defined corporate personality. As I always advise my clients....*if it touches the customer, it's a marketing issue.*™

And nothing, nothing touches your customers more than how he or she perceives your corporate image.

This makes the management of your corporate image one of the most potent marketing and management tools available for senior executives and business owners to use in ensuring the viable execution of your corporate vision.

Key Point: everything an organization does, and does not do, has an impact on its corporate image.

Taking Action: ask your senior managers to brainstorm and develop a list of the things your organization does that has a positive impact on your corporate image, and a list of the things you do that has (or could have) a negative impact on your corporate image. What can you do to leverage the positive things? What can you do to eliminate the negative ones?

What does your organization stand for?

Where is it headed?

What are its core strengths, traditions, and principles? Are these found within your corporate image, as *perceived* by your key constituents?

Survey your customers on their *perceptions* of your corporate brand image. Ask if your corporate brand adds value to your product and service brands.

Brand Name Strategies

When it comes to branding strategies, there are three approaches you can take.

These are: the mega name strategy, the dual name strategy, and the product brand name strategy. Let me explain by giving illustrations of each.

Kodak, Sony, LG, and IBM are good examples of the mega brand name strategy. They rarely bother to develop product branding, preferring to have all of their products closely identified with the corporate brand.

The dual naming strategy is where the corporate brand name is used in close conjunction with the product brand name. Nestle, F+N, and Heinz are typical companies that use the dual brand name strategy. There's Nestle Nescafe, the Nestle Crunch candy bar, and other Nestle products. For F+N, we find F+N Fruit Tree drinks, F+N Soya bean, F+N tonic water, etc.

The last strategy is the product brand name strategy, used by Proctor & Gamble, Unilever, Colgate and others. Here, the customer often doesn't know which company makes the particular brands they are using. And, quite frankly, the customer really doesn't care, as long as their Head & Shoulders shampoo, their Close-Up toothpaste, or their particular laundry detergent remains consistently satisfying.

None of these three naming strategies is inherently better than the others. And you are by no means limited to the use of just one branding strategy. For instance, even Sony used the dual naming strategy when it developed the portable music player years ago and branded it the Sony Walkman. Which strategy or strategies you use is up to you and your particular business and industry situation.

However, since the corporate image is one of the most powerful marketing tools available to you....the better your corporate image is to your customers....the more you may want to ensure that your corporate brand is closely associated with your product brands.

As your competitors cannot copy or mimic a well-defined corporate personality, the management of your corporate image may be the most strategic marketing weapon available to you.

Key Points: since the corporate image is one of the most powerful marketing tools available to you, you may want to ensure that your corporate brand is closely associated with your product brands.

Taking Action: can your product brands benefit from your corporate brand image? Why or why not?

Is there a possibility that your product brands could damage the core corporate brand reputation? How? What would be the likely effects on your ability to grow your business if this was to occur? What preventive steps can you put into place now?

What is your well-defined corporate personality? Would your customers agree with this definition? Does your corporate brand provide you with any competitive advantages? If not, this needs serious investigation.

The Value of a Good Corporate Brand

Let's return once again to the subject of corporate image.

As I was conducting the research for my first book — *Corporate Image Management: A Marketing Discipline For the 21st Century*, I began looking for illustrations to prove the value of a strong corporate image.

I knew intuitively that a strong corporate image would provide several levels of value to an organization — such as financial value, market place value, human resource value and, of course, customer value.

But how to prove this?

Well, an example from the automotive world probably best illustrates the market value of a powerful corporate brand.

In the late 1980s, Toyota and General Motors created a joint venture company in Freemont, California that was called New United Motor Manufacturing Inc. (NUMMI). The plant produced two identical cars, the Toyota Corolla and the General Motors Geo Prizm.

These two cars were produced on the same manufacturing line, using the same raw materials....the same labor....the same manufacturing process....basically the same everything. In the computer world we would call these two car models "pin-for-pin compatible."

The only difference between the two models was that some of them carried the Toyota Corolla brand name and some of them had the General Motors GM Geo Prizm marque.

Being almost identical, they sold for approximately the same price and depreciated at about the same rate, correct?

One would think so. But in fact they did not. The Toyota Corolla sold in 1989 for about 10% more than the GM Geo Prizm. It then depreciated more slowly than the Geo Prizm, resulting in a second-hand value almost 18% higher than the American-branded model after five years.

Why the differences? One has to conclude that the relative strength of the Toyota brand and corporate name, over the General Motors name, in the late 1980s played the first significant role. If car buyers perceived a Toyota named car to be superior to a GM car in the same model class, they would be willing to pay a higher sticker price.

But that wasn't the entire difference, according to a study by the Boston Consulting Group. The BCG study reported that the after-sales service provided by the Toyota dealer network sustained, and even boosted, the perceived edge of the Toyota name.

In other words, the corporate image *management* process taken by Toyota to ensure that the service departments at its dealer network wouldn't tarnish or deteriorate the Toyota brand helped to reinforce the positive attributes of the Toyota identity. These had already given it an edge in the marketplace vis-à-vis a direct competitor brand manufactured in the same facility, using the same materials and labor. This example shows the direct value of a powerful and well-managed corporate brand.

And it was stories such as this, as I continued to conduct my research into the value of corporate branding and corporate image management, which led me to conclude that corporate image management is one of the most powerful and potent marketing and management tools available to senior executives and business owners.

Key Point: corporate image *management* is one of the most powerful marketing and management tools available.

Taking Action: what are your *internal* processes for managing your corporate brand and corporate image?

How does your after-sales service affect the way your organization is perceived by customers, prospects, and other interested parties?

What's the weakest link in your corporate image management chain?   What steps can be taken immediately to strengthen this weakest link?

What's the strongest aspect of your corporate image? How can this be further leveraged to develop market leadership for your products or services?

Hurting Corporate Brand Image

We have been discussing the power of corporate image management and how this is one of the most powerful and potent marketing and management tools available to senior executives and business owners as they lead their organizations.

Management of the corporate image is a key component of change management. But what often needs changing or modifying is not how the corporate logo appears or is used, but several other aspects of the organization's visual communications to its audiences.

Many of these other visual components go entirely unnoticed, until a proper and sweeping visual audit of the organization's corporate identity practices is conducted.

To illustrate, here are some of the image damaging conditions that have been discovered on corporate image management projects in which this consultant and writer was personally involved:

- ◆ A publicly listed manufacturing concern had left a broken window pane not replaced for a period of at least six months, yet it did not understand why its messages on its new quality improvement initiatives were not believed by security analysts. (It was obvious to me that they did not walk their talk.)

♦ Another manufacturer preached a policy of treating all employees equally and putting customers first. Interestingly, however, the only reserved vehicle parking space in the entire company was directly in front of the main entrance. The spot was reserved for the firm's CEO, who was transported around Singapore in his chauffeur-driven car. Both employees and customers had to walk carefully around his vehicle to enter the main lobby as there was not much space between the car and the front doors. Since he was dropped off at the front door anyway, there really wasn't any need, except for ego satisfaction, for his luxury marque to be positioned at the main entrance. So much for equality among employees and consideration for customers.

♦ For some reason, companies like to place their logos everywhere, but this is not really necessary. For instance, one company I visited had its logo and name painted (by hand) on the large trash containers placed around its manufacturing facility. And the lids for these waste bins were *chained* to steel pipes.

I never learned if this meant that the organization's management did not trust the staff not to steal its huge trash cans, but I did convince them that it probably wasn't a good idea for customers and security analysts visiting the plant to see the company's name emblazoned so prominently on trash receptacles.

♦ One multinational bank had only three branches in a particular Asian market, but was using four different advertising agencies and graphics design companies to produce its marketing communications materials. It was little wonder that the various products and services on offer from this bank showed little visual resemblance to each other, though the corporate logo was consistently used in all materials thanks to a very detailed graphics standards manual produced by global headquarters. But its overall marketing communications and product brand messages were muddied by the inconsistency in overall approach and tonality.

♦ A major retailer of fine, upscale watches prided itself on having one of the most complete ranges of premium watches available in its outlets. However, it could not understand why traffic into its stores were below expectations, until it was pointed out that the glass doors to each store featured decals and labels for every credit card and discount card imaginable. Anyone paying thousands of dollars for a watch was not going to be enticed into the purchase just because they could use a plastic payment card or a discount card. Once the decals were removed and the aluminum frames around the doors changed to quality-looking teak, both traffic levels and sales volumes increased in all outlets.

What constitutes a corporate brand? In a word: everything.

Everything an organization does, and does not do, communicates a message about its corporate image.

As a result, you really cannot afford to overlook, or ignore, the need to continually monitor and manage your corporate image.

Key Point: what constitutes a corporate brand? In a word: everything.

Taking Action: Corporate Image Management is not a one-off "exercise" or something that gets tackled yearly during the annual marketing plan cycle. What are you and your managers doing *today* to monitor and manage your corporate image?

Do you have a core set of corporate values? How are these communicated to customers? How are these communicated and inculcated in new hires?

What are the three most important characteristics of your corporate brand? What actions is the organization taking that might harm or damage these characteristics? How can you be sure such actions will no longer take place?

Corporate Identity vs. Corporate Image

We have been writing about the importance of corporate image and what makes this such an important management and marketing tool in helping to ensure the future success of your organization.

Today, I am going to highlight some of the important differences between corporate *image* and corporate *identity*.

Jenny Bigio, who led a design firm in Singapore called Write-Angles, has an interesting way of describing the importance of the corporate identity system to clients.

"Imagine," she says, "wearing the same outfit to work all day, every day, year in and year out. An outfit that must differentiate you from everyone else on this planet. An outfit that defines your character. An outfit that communicates all facets of your personality in a clear compelling way. An outfit that attracts and keeps the right people in your orbit. An outfit that is as uniquely yours as your thumbprint."

"That," she concludes, "is the essence of corporate imaging. Like one's own DNA imprint, no two organizations are exactly the same. The corporate image manifests in a visual and verbal identity that is your mark of recognition. It is the 'outfit' that is the expression of your organization's unique personality."

Hers is an apt description of corporate identity. The corporate identity system is the visual representation and graphic style of an organization, usually taking the form of a corporate signature combined with a corporate symbol or logo. These are used to visually and graphically distinguish the organization from its competitors and to visually and graphically differentiate the enterprise in the global marketplace through a consistent use of typeface, color palette, and logo identifier.

The corporate identity system is the primary expression of how the organization views itself, and is also crucial to the relationship building process with customers, prospects, employees, potential employees, business partners, the general public, shareholders, and your other key constituents.

Through the corporate identity system the organization is saying to these constituents: *this is who we are.*

In essence, the corporate identity is the one way any organization makes its soul, character, personality, and collective culture visible to the outside world.

However, it is important to note that the corporate identity is only *one component* of a well-managed corporate image.

The design approach to corporate identity development, which has historically been the traditional methodology to corporate image creation, provides only temporary and short-lived benefits.

In today's world, however, corporate identity development alone is no longer sufficient. As your organization moves toward a marketing excellence based on dialogue excellence and relationship excellence with core customers, the corporate image of the organization must be managed more closely and diligently.

Management is the most important word in the phrase corporate image management. In the design approach, the words image and identity would be more important because the final objective is the creation of a projected image.

With the strategic approach to corporate image management, there is no final destiny or objective. The process of continuous management is both the methodology and the destination.

In short, management of the corporate image goes hand in hand with the development and management of the organization's corporate strategy. The key here is that the corporate image management process forces you to continuously define the singular message that describes how the organization is different — and better — than its rivals.

Unlike the design-driven corporate identity process, however, the unifying message derived from corporate image management practices will be equally valid to all key constituents, not just to customers and competitors.

Better still, the external projection and communication of the principles, values, and beliefs underlying the corporate image (the corporate soul) will be based on individual and collective action, not on a shrewdly created positioning tagline.

Corporate image management: a true marketing discipline. Need we say more?

Key Point: the corporate *identity* is only one component of a well-managed corporate image.

Taking Action: ask your key managers to write one sentence each on the soul, character, personality, and culture of your organization. How similar are these sentences? How greatly do they differ? Do they appear to all talk about the same organization? Is it time for a little refresher among management about your core values and what your organization stands for and represents?

The process of continuous management is both the methodology and the destination for the corporate image management process. What steps have you taken lately to manage this process?

What is the single message that describes how your organization is different, and better, than your rivals? What actions need to be taken to give greater support *today* to this singular message?

Corporate Image as a Strategic Weapon

How powerful is corporate image as a strategic weapon?

To find out, let's consider the process someone with only limited knowledge or experience of a particular product line goes through when they need to make a purchase decision.

I will use wine as our product category of choice, because most people have only a limited knowledge of the choices available and most are unfamiliar with the specific criteria that differentiates wine styles and wine makers.

Plus, the selection process is complicated by many factors: the need to match wine style with food choices; ambience; suitability and acceptability to the diners; and, of course, pricing.

Add to this the knowledge that the choice will reflect upon the person making the selection — and the decision becomes more difficult and complex.

The goal, for anyone faced with the problem of wine selection, is to choose an appropriate bottle at an acceptable price, two criteria that change as the situation changes.

Hence, the buyer must rely on:

- Previous experience or familiarity with the products found on the wine menu.

- Suggestions or recommendations by the wine steward or waiter.

- Perceptions of the wine region, bottle labels, or grape varietals on offer.

If unfamiliar with the wines in stock, and in the absence of reliable help from the wine steward or waiter, the buyer must rely totally upon perceptions of the products on offer and the ratio of price to image.

For years, the public image of France as a quality producer of wines was strong enough for French wines to win many, if not most, of the marketing battles just described.

Today, equally strong images for Australian and Californian wines have made the purchase decision-making process more difficult for the average consumer. Fortunately, the quality of wines from these regions, and other regions such as South Africa, New Zealand, and even Chile, is sufficiently high that our hypothetical wine buyer can hardly go wrong these days.

Even so, the reputation of labels such as Penfolds Grange from Australia and Château Margaux from France allows them to command premium prices vintage after vintage.

If anyone doubts the power of the corporate image as a strategic marketing weapon, they should study the relationship between wine prices and the public perceptions of the names found on the labels of the premium priced bottles. Wines made directly across the road from one another, from grapes grown on similar soils, in the same climate, at the same time, and harvested in the same manner can differ by anywhere from 10% to 500% in pricing.

For the past two to three decades, the basic principles of marketing have been taught as the four Ps: product, price, promotion, and place.

While their importance is still undisputed, the formula of the 4Ps is now only partly sufficient. Formerly considered merely as part of "promotion," the image perception of a company, brand, or product has become ever more important in the marketing success equation.

For proof, consider the immediate global success of numerous branded goods and corporations whose names did not exist in the general lexicon until their brand creations: names like Adidas, Nike, Compaq, Motorola, Nokia, Kodak, and Pixar.

The new equation for marking success is:

The 4Ps combined with Corporate Image Management equals success.

Alternatively, this can be thought of as the five Ps of marketing, with **perception** joining the ranks of product, price, promotion, and place.

When you start adding the perception of your corporate image to your marketing success formula, you will quickly understand why corporate image management as a strategic marketing weapon is nothing less than the cutting edge of marketing and management technology.

Key Point: corporate image management is a strategic weapon required for marketing success.

Taking Action: evaluate how your corporate image is perceived by customers, prospects, and other constituents. Does this perception differ by group?

What are the positive characteristics of your corporate image? What are the negative ones?

Can the negative ones be eliminated or reduced? How? Can the positive ones be leveraged further?

What could be the effect on your market share, your ability to increase margins, and your opportunities for enhanced relationships with customers if the perception of your corporate image was improved?

How can the perception of your corporate image be improved through corporate behavior (not through advertising and other communications programs)?

The Impact of Corporate Image on Your Communications

In our book on corporate image management, which classifies this management tool as a key marketing discipline, we introduced the concept of perception as the 5th "P" of marketing.

We called it perception, rather than positioning, because one of the weaknesses with the four basic Ps of marketing (product, price, place, and promotion) is that these four are typical viewed from the perspective of the corporation or organization. And looking at corporate image as a positioning strategy would have repeated this error.

Hence, by understanding that nothing touches the customer more than how he or she *perceives* your corporate image, corporate leaders, business owners, and marketing professionals are forced to look at the world through the eyes of their customers and other critical constituents.

This thinking also has a major impact on how organizations communicate with their customers, employees, partners, and other important constituents.

Marketers and marketing professionals have long spoken and written about communications as being the lifeblood of the marketing process. All four key elements of the marketing process (product, price, promotion, and place) are driven by the organization's ability to communicate effectively and convincingly about these four factors.

Through the years, new forms of marketing communications have been devised and field tested: advertising, public relations, promotions, coupons, sponsorships, direct mail, telemarketing, and now today's hottest areas of activity — websites and social media.

The primary purpose of these activities has been, and still is, to inform the targeted audience about certain characteristics or properties of the organization, product, or service. As such, the vast majority of worldwide marketing communications expenditures still remain in one-way communication activities, with messages being sent in one direction by marketers to their intended audiences.

The response mechanism used for tracking this type of communication process has largely been sales figures. If product unit sales rose immediately after the marketing communications efforts appeared, then the campaign was considered to have enjoyed some level of success.

As this puts a great burden on the designers and implementers of all forms of marketing communications, another school of thought — the importance of raising awareness as a prelude to sales — entered the marketing scene. The argument here is that potential customers need to become aware of the product or service first, particularly for considered and expensive purchases.

The response mechanism in this case has been broadened to include pre- and post-campaign awareness research studies, telephone enquiries, customer traffic flows in showrooms, direct response requests for additional literature or more information, and the number of "hits" on the website home page or the number of social media followers.

All of these remain valid measurement criteria for tracking the return on marketing communications expenditures for organizations trapped in the trenches of positioning excellence warfare.

Moving forward, however, the marketing communications process will take a giant leap for organizations entering the relationship excellence marketing arena. These organizations will quickly learn that marketing communications needs to be a two-way, mutually beneficial umbilical cord *with* their relationship partners — also known as customers.

By adding the 5th "P" of marketing — that being perception — to the marketing equation, organizations will begin to comprehend that the perceived image of the organization by its customers and other important constituents is one of the most important filters in the communications process.

Everything your organization is currently doing is already communicating to each of your intended and unintended audiences. To ensure that the right messages are being communicated *and* received, the organization must put into place the most powerful marketing discipline available — the corporate image management process.

Key Point: everything your organization is currently doing communicates to each of your intended and unintended audiences.

Taking Action: are you constantly and consistently communicating messages that reinforce the perception of your core corporate values by your intended and unintended audiences?

Are your communications efforts focused on "positioning" or "perception?" Do you see the world from only your own organizational perspective, or also from the perspective of your key constituents (both internal and external)?

How does the perception of your corporate image filter the other messages, such as product brand messages, that the organization is sending?

Leading Change through the Corporate Image Management Process (Part One)

One of the most challenging issues facing senior executives, business owners, and entrepreneurs today is how to manage and lead change.

Can you manage change?

If you cannot, it will manage you. And none of us would want that inscription on our corporate tombstones.

In truth, however, you cannot truly *manage* change. Change management is a misnomer. Change cannot be managed. Change must be *led*.

Trying to manage change means reacting. Leading change requires pro-active mental and physical states, combined with a sense of purpose, a spirit of optimism, and an ability to communicate plans and goals.

To properly lead change, however one must have more than the gift of gab and power of inspiration. One needs a set of powerful change tools, and the best implements to include in the corporate change tool set are:

Vision statement — the ideal future state of the organization and the place it would like to find itself (and its customers) at some destined point in time. Note that neither of these may ever be achieved, but that is not a problem. Sometimes the vision will change over time. In other cases it may be a never-ending goal, like a person's desire to be "the best parent possible."

Mission statement — a stated and measurable set of desired outcomes that should be achievable, understandable, believable, specific, time-bound, and relevant to customers as well as to staff. At the same time, the goals should stretch the organization to accomplish and perform consistently at levels that surpass current output and results; exceed customer satisfaction criteria and employee satisfaction levels; and that build, maintain, and enhance customer and business partner relationships.

Corporate culture — one that fosters individual and organizational growth in line with the vision and mission statements. The corporate culture will help to ensure that individual and collective patterns of behavior consistently enhance relationships with customers, prospects, business partners, and other key influential audiences.

Marketing strategy — one that is customer focused and that drives the organization to identify and monitor changing customer needs, to create and deliver value-added solutions to these needs, to understand relationship requirements of customer and business partners, and to establish a basis and framework for relationship development and perpetuation. The marketing strategy should be the underlying business driver for organizations, not the quarterly or yearly financial goals.

Market perception — a clearly definable understanding by key target audiences of who and what the organization is, where it is heading, and why it is relevant. This perception must be consistently projected through both the organization's communications and its corporate behavior patterns. These need to reinforce one another, resulting in unified and solidified messages that are clearly perceived by those who interact with the organization.

The tool that unifies these five elements — the vision statement, the mission statement, the corporate culture, the marketing strategy, and the market perception of the organization — into a holistic corporate change mechanism is the corporate image management process.

Manage and lead the corporate image, and the organization is more likely to accomplish the tasks and goals desired of it by its leaders and stakeholders.

Corporate image management always focuses on the process. This enables management to lead the overall direction of the organization, providing in-built flexibility for maneuvering through changing conditions, rather than emphasizing specific targets or goals.

By keeping the corporate image management goal visionary, the on-going corporate image management process provides corporate leaders with a tool for dealing with the unpredictable future.

And that is a much better inscription for any leader than one that says he or she couldn't manage change.

Key Point: the tool that unifies the five key elements of change leadership into a holistic corporate change mechanism is the corporate image management process.

Taking Action: when was the last time your vision statement, mission statement, corporate culture, marketing strategy, and market perception of the organization were all thoroughly analyzed and evaluated? These are not items cast in stone, but rather very important facets of your corporate image that need continuous evaluation, understanding, and management.

How can you and your department do a better job of helping to lead the overall organization through change?

Is your marketing strategy customer focused or product based? What gains could you make from becoming more customer focused in your marketing strategy?

When was the last time you surveyed your employees to see if your corporate goals and tasks are fully understood, believed, and appear achievable to them? What responses might you uncover if you surveyed them today? How could clearer communication of these goals and tasks help lead to a higher probability of accomplishment?

Leading Change through the Corporate Image Management Process (Part Two)

In recent years, management practices related to change have covered the entire spectrum from "if it ain't broke, don't fix it" to "change everything from top to bottom."

The re-engineering processes of the early 1990s ran the gamut from changing internal processes and procedures to re-inventing the organization by throwing away practically everything (and almost everyone) including the proverbial kitchen sink.

Unfortunately, such practices approach the corporate entity as an inanimate object and the relationships with customers as inorganic inclinations.

But an organization — especially your organization — is not an inanimate object and its valued relationships with customers, partners, and others need not be temporary tendencies subject to changing whims and passing penchants.

In fact, the corporate body should be thought of as an individual's body. One can rarely fix the health problems associated with being overweight merely by going on a diet. Rather, all the tools available to the individual need to be used: dieting, changing activity levels, exercise, modifying eating habits and the types of foods eaten, removing or managing causes of stress, etc.

The same applies to corporations and organizations. Those who wish to lead change should use all of the elements in the corporate change tool box, not merely one or two of the most obvious gadgets. The blueprint for how to effectively use these tools lies within the corporate image management process.

Leadership during times of change is mandatory. This segue in marketing excellence to the new era of relationship excellence is exactly the kind of change that will require astute organizational leadership.

The leadership of change, however, cannot exist solely at the top of the organizational pyramid structure. Change leadership, particularly in terms of corporate image management and relationship excellence, must exist throughout the organization at all levels.

When planned, change can be good — for the organization as a whole, for its individual employee members, and for its relationships with key constituencies in the market place. Using the corporate image management process during times of change provides the organization with the strongest set of tools for executives to use in leading and implementing change. It provides an understanding of how the organization perceives its marketing environment, how the market place perceives the organization, and what criteria key audiences will use in their decision-making processes about relationships.

Given that change is inevitable, continuous, unstoppable, and occurring at a faster pace than ever before, the key issue for organizational leaders is whether they want to react to change in a crisis mode or in a prepared and planned manner.

The change agenda can be set by the global forces of the market environment, by your better prepared and equipped competitors, or through your own organization's readiness and willingness to take the lead.

When you embark upon the latter course, the corporate image management process enables you to identify and exploit the experiences, foresight, creativity, customer knowledge, and enthusiasm that exists throughout your organization.

In short, corporate image management is a wonderful tool for executive leadership and business owners, particularly suited to today's changing times.

Key Point: change leadership, particularly in terms of corporate image management and relationship excellence, must exist throughout the organization at all levels.

Taking Action: how prepared for change are you? Where does change leadership take place in your organization, only at the top or throughout the organization?

What change leadership skills does the organization need to develop in order to become better prepared for change leadership?

How can the corporate image management process be used to lead and implement change within your organization?

About the Author

Steven Howard
Author, Marketing and Branding Strategist

Steven Howard is a leading marketing strategist, positioning specialist, consultant, and author whose stellar marketing and sales career in Asia, Australia, and the USA has covered a wide variety of fields, ranging from consumer electronics to publishing and from a national airline to personal financial products.

Founder of **Howard Marketing Services**, he has consulted to companies in the financial services, education, industrial products, consumer products, restaurants, petroleum, publishing, and hospitality fields. In 2014 he was named to a list of the Global Top 100 SEO Copywriters.

He is the author of 10 other books:

Corporate Image Management: A Marketing Discipline

Powerful Marketing Minutes: 50 Ways to Develop Market Leadership

MORE Powerful Marketing Minutes: 50 New Ways to Develop Market Leadership

Asian Words of Wisdom

Asian Words of Knowledge

Essential Asian Words of Wisdom

Pillars of Growth: Strategies for Leading Sustainable Growth (co-author with three others)

Motivation Plus Marketing Equals Money (co-author with four others)

Marketing Words of Wisdom

The Best of the Monday Morning Marketing Memo

He also writes the *Monday Morning Marketing Memo*, *The Steven Howard Marketing Blog*, and the *Keeping Good Customers Blog*.

Contact Details
Email: steven@howard-marketing.com

Twitter: @stevenbhoward

LinkedIn: www.linkedin.com/in/stevenbhoward

Facebook: facebook.com/MondayMorningMarketingMemo

Facebook: facebook.com/HowardMarketingServices

Website: www.howard-marketing.com

Blog: www.StevenHowardMarketingBlog.com

www.ingramcontent.com/pod-product-compliance
Lightning Source LLC
Chambersburg PA
CBHW070923210326
41520CB00021B/6779